WATER UNDER THE NUMBER 4 BRIDGE

Water Under the Number 4 Bridge
A Memoir of the Beacon Years (1988-1993)

Susan Engle Roquemore

Water Under the Number 4 Bridge

Copyright © Susan Engle Roquemore 2015

All rights reserved. This book or any portion thereof may not be reproduced or used in any manner whatsoever without the express written permission of the publisher except for the use of brief quotations in a book review.

Photographs are those of the author.

Printed in the United States of America

First Printing 2015

To all my Cedar Key ghosts and to David,
who keeps those ghosts alive in my memory

CONTENTS

Preface
    A Voice from the Twilight Zone   1
Part One
    Water Under the Number 4 Bridge   5
    The Cast of Characters   7
    Cedar Key Then and Now   9
    A Little More About Us   11
    Mother "Touched" by Ceremony   23
    A Story Never Told   24
Part Two
    On Newspapers & Writing   29
        New Weekly Newspaper Debuts   31
        Beacon to Become a "Mom & Pop" Operation   31
        At Home in the Fourth Estate   32
        Inky Veins Inspires Writer   33
        September Song   36
        Dear Robin, Wish You Were Here   37
        If We Have Stepped on Any Toes   38
        Commentary   39
        Write Right   41
        My Life as a Syntax Error   43
        Did John Steinbeck Have My Problems?   45
        Mamas, Don't Let Your Babies Grow Up To Be Writers (Let Them Be Accountants or Cowboys, or Such)   47
    Cedar Key Living   49
        How Do You Find Cedar Key?   51
        Plenty to Do in Cedar Key   52
        Another Side of the Mailbox   54
        If This Is Fantasyland, I'm Sure Not Sleeping Beauty   55
        Our Own Little Blood Factory   56
        What a Good Idea   57
        There's a World Between a Visitor and a Tourist   59
        This Was the Week that Was (and Is)   61
        Tuning In to Festival Sights and Sounds   63
        White Powder   64
        Lost in Downtown Cedar Key   65
        I Want to Vote in Cedar Key   66
        Old Dogs, New Tricks, There's No Place Like Home   68

Cedar Key Living (continued)
- The Pelican Brief — 70
- A Letter to the Editor — 71
- Animal Control — 71
- Those Dear Deer on Highway 24 — 73
- "Looney Tunes," and Other Things I Wish I'd Written — 74
- Sunrise, Sunset, Cedar Key — 76

A Picture Album — 77

In the Middle of History — 89
- As the Wind Blows — 91
- The Adventures of a Museum Buff — 93
- Historical Society on Annual Seahorse Trek — 94
- John Muir — 96
- Is It Too Much Too Soon, or Too Little Too Late? — 99
- Another Cedar Key Convert — 100

Getting Outside — 103
- Lettuce See Now — 105
- Summer in the Cedar Key Garden — 106
- Did You Ever Sit on a Cactus? — 108
- Rose Gardens and Grape Arbors — 109
- Spring Has Sprung — 111
- An Ooga-Ooga Horn Wouldn't Hurt This Biker — 113
- Of Sails and Seas — 115
- Canoes to You Too — 116
- Fishing Licenses, Fines and Funny Business — 118
- Low Tide in Cedar Key — 120

Travels With Mr. Dave — 123
- Every Which Way but There — 125
- Touring Highways and Byways? Helps To Be in Love — 129
- You Take Me to the Nicest Places — 131
- Day Tripping Around and About — 133
- Adventure Doesn't Have to Include Achy-Breaky Bones, Muscles or Credit Cards — 135
- Hip-Hip-Hippodrome — 139

My Life in Cedar Key Time — 141
- Wonderful Ideas (That Didn't Work) — 143
- When the Merry-Go-Round (and Everything Else) Broke Down — 145
- The Light of My Life — 147
- It's a Lost Cause—Losing the Right Stuff — 148
- Oops . . . I Just Had It — 150

My Life in Cedar Key Time (continued)
   Spring Cleaning Can Be Traumatic   151
   Can This Room Be Saved?   153
   Dirt Just Happens   155
   Living and Loving the House Guest   156
   Will the Patron Saint of Transmissions
     Please Stand Up   157
   Don't Forget to Wear Clean Underwear   158
   Incredible? You'd Better Believe It   161

Edibles   165
   How to Stuff a Wild Manicotti   167
   Some Cooking Memories   168
   Kid's Kooking Korner   170
   Children Should Understand the "Mother Syndrome"   172
   Blame It on the Italians   173
   In Quest of the Holy Grille   175
   On Cannery Row   177
   Oysters—You Just Can't Stop   180
   To Catch a Crab   181
   Cedar Key Simmers Some Chowder   183
   The Taste of Success—First Annual Cedar
     Key Chowder Cook-Off a Hit   184
   Diary of a Bean Queen   186

Weather or Not   189
   Snowflake of Cedar Key   191
   Whither the Weatherman   193
   Saving for a Rainy Day   194
   Rainy Day Woman   195
   Do Like They Do in Georgia . . . About the
     Weather, That Is   198

A Final Word   203
   A Fine Farewell   204
   My Last Letter to the *Beacon*   205

Preface

Cedar Key Dock Street at sunset—1985

Water Under the Number 4 Bridge

A Voice from the Twilight Zone: 32625

No one just passes through Cedar Key, Florida. Indeed, it has been said that no one ever really leaves it, either. The sounds of her silence, the subtle mewlings of her breezes, the outrageous howl of her storms, the smells of the sea, and tactile temptations keep the soul in limbo if the body strays.

Cedar Key, the town, is a living, breathing, belching, wind-breaking place. One chooses his pace on the island. One chooses his voice, his face. If there is a unique quality here in Small-Town, Florida, it is that freedom of choice: almost a frontier spirit. There is a ferocity among her residents to protect her and keep her healthy in body and soul: *mens sano in corpore sano*. It is at once a sepulcher of old Indian bones and pottery and old American industry and an ant-hill of mischievous developers spitting phraseology with environmentalists. It is a sea of oystermen, offering grist for hungry and not so hungry artists and writers.

Cedar Key is home. Perhaps, it has always been my home.

There was this column published in the *Cedar Key Beacon* called "Impressions Of An Island Lifestyle." I wrote it for five years until I became more of a mountain trail recluse than an island castaway. It really didn't seem to matter to my readers whether I was extolling the sunrises over the sea or the sun setting behind a rocky tor: it was the "islands of my mind" that they explored with me.

Abiding friendships evolved from the writing of that column for which I am eternally grateful. I made a few enemies as well. Even my mother got mad at me once. My husband was called a "saint" for living with me and my children couldn't wait to see what *lies* I'd told about them that week. An aunt chided me for my irreverence. Most of all, I found that I could allow people to chuckle with me over the foibles that all of us experience: laughter and tears, frustrations and fears. In the course of writing this column, I found that I no longer had to resort to hyperbole to make people laugh: life was funny enough without exaggeration. In the darkest hours, there is always a sense of irony and at the very least, a sardonic humor.

No laugh track accompanies this book. Neither is it high

drama. It won't send you to the last page to see "Who Dun It?"

What it is, then, is a book of maundering and meandering thoughts that overnight were embraced by the townspeople and visitors; that brought letters of glee and outrage from every corner of subscriptiondom.

The purpose of this book, if not to bring about great guffaws of laughter, is to help you smile once in awhile at human foible and to frown at some human frailty.

It's not a book that could be made into a movie: there are just too many sets and too many characters, and the cast keeps changing and the set keeps moving.

Most of the vignettes first appeared in the *Cedar Key Beacon*. Some were stashed in the bottom drawer. Some were composed as letters or for special people. And some were written simply to glue this book together, because, as with islands, the sands of my mind are always shifting.

Bringing all of this together into a workable text was no mean feat. We were not talking recipes here. The theme is only life itself and living it, believing in it and loving it: Pure rich joys and hearty anger, frustration bordering on the clouds with only purple linings. Plums have purple linings! Didn't you know?

It's a book meant to have the pages dog-eared and the cover have coffee rings. It's a book that you can read to a friend a page from over the phone. It's the type of thing you can leave out on the coffee table and let the kids know you are reading. *Again.*

This book is not intended as a literary masterpiece. I'm not Erma Bombeck. I'm not Dave Barry. I'm not Jean Kerr. But I admire all three for their contributions to helping us all lighten up a bit and laugh at ourselves. The book is not meant as slapstick comedy, but some of the routines could have been used on "I Love Lucy." I lead that kind of life.

Reading this book will require the wearing of your time-travel glasses. Except for occasional editorial comments, the articles were written over twenty years ago, when Cedar Key and indeed Florida were perhaps a shade different and more innocent.

Part One

Cedar Key Seafoods Building—1985

I
Water Under the Number 4 Bridge

It is entirely understandable that you may not be familiar with the bridge of the title or its waters. The Number 4 is the first bridge you will cross if you venture into Cedar Key from the land side. It is probably the way most people meet the island today. The bridge is officially named the "Randolph Hodges Bridge." The name Number Four refers, unromantically, to the name of the channel which it spans.

The saline waters under the bridge are subject to tides, sharing space with Waccasassa Bay on the east side and the Gulf of Mexico to the west. I have no idea which water is which and just where they become the admixture. It's someplace around that bridge. Twice a day, usually, the tide is high and twice a day the tide is low—usually. Sometimes it is *really high* and sometimes it is *really low*. The meteorologists can't seem to predict Cedar Key tides or weather. Maybe God can but God isn't telling. Today, there is an old fishing pier that juts out parallel to the highway. It is a remnant of the older road that spanned the Number 4 Channel. This road was wooden and made a clack-clack sound under wheels. Folks who remember that old road still get misty eyed remembering that special coming-home sound. For latter day residents, the smell of home is usually enough. There is an earthy smell—no, the smell is salty, fishy, an odor of rotting vegetation that is like attar of roses to those who call the island home. Dogs bark and cats meow and jump to car windows long before they experience the bridge in an automobile. Humans just sigh. Shoulders relax and tension flows outward faster than the sun can set on the horizon.

Lest you think this is paradise with a zip code, I hasten to explain that it is miserably hot in the summer, windy and cold in the winter, has bugs that the rest of Florida hasn't even heard of. The soil is sand-laced with pelican guano fit only for sandspurs and creeping eruption. We have fire ants, and no-see-ums (a frightful midge that thinks it is a flying alligator). Our beaches are made up of razor-sharp oyster bars. The sand is ugly and gray. The storms we experience are world-class. The hardwood trees are gnarled scrub oaks. Our pines have an infestation of Japanese beetles. We have a school so small that it is threatened with closure every few years. You probably don't want to risk your sanity living on an island that is best known for its place on the hurricane maps of Florida. If you do venture across the Number 4 Bridge, expect nothing. Nobody cares if you are on the island unless you molest a child, a dog or neighbor cat or speed across a bridge. Nobody will bother you or invite you to join a church or an organization. You will be on your own. It's not that the people aren't friendly. Indeed, Cedar Keyans are the friendliest people in the world—they just figure you are here for your own reasons—which is none of their business. That attitude, so prevalent in the 1980's into the 1990's, is changing. There are people who now see dollar signs when they see a newcomer. (How absolutely revolting I find this new friendliness!)

There was a day when I too was a newcomer. I will try to reconstruct that short period of time with the least amount of sogginess. I tend to be less than poetic when explaining my (our) first days, weeks, months in Cedar Key as full-time residents. I've always been cursed with an excellent memory but times and places are always colored by feelings. Those impressions were the subject of my weekly newspaper columns. I look back at those pages today as if they happened yesterday. The child in school is eighteen once again. The trees are seedlings. My hair is still mousey brown—not senior-citizen silver. I don't wear fake fingernails. My cat's name is Shadow and he is still a youngster—not now years in a Virginia grave. My mother is still my mother and Daddy is still with me. Husband Dave's parents are very much part of our lives. I have no daughters-in-law or grand-children. I have yet to take my first serious long-distance hike. It would be years before I found Mount Katahdin in Maine on foot the first time.

We crossed the Number 4 Bridge to stay August 13, 1987.

II
The Cast of Characters

As we meander through the years of my columns and my memories, we will bump into some colorful characters. My favorite subjects over the years were my family. The most favorite subject of all was my husband David. He called himself "Fang." David achieved a bit of street fame as the foil to my sense of humor.

Dave and I have been blessed over the years. We still find the other fun to be around. He's just a little smarter than me. (I can do crossword puzzles better!) Our childhoods were fairly different, but the refrain of family unity and loyalty was always there for both of us. We like flea markets and junk stores and almost anything old, including each other. Neither of us is hidebound to remember gifts on birthdays, but we love giving gifts when the spirit moves us, whether these are diamonds or daisies.

I tried to be more careful with other family members. On one very memorable occasion I made my own dear mother angry with me for poking fun at the way she traveled—talking to every Tom, Dick and Harry at every truck stop and intersection and rest area between here and Atlanta, Georgia. Mama was like that. I never lied about anyone but I might have stretched the facts just a little bit. As the years went on, I found less cause for hyperbole. In Cedar Key, truth is generally stranger than any story I could make up.

I didn't have to be too careful with the cats—they would love me or not regardless.

It was the days of veneration of Erma Bombeck and I was her Number One acolyte. My children did cause me decades of post postpartum depression. I learned to cook the Bombeck Way: Put an onion in the oven at 4 PM and break out the TV dinners an hour later. A few years later I took up cooking as serious fun but for those years it was a minimalist endeavor. I lived by the crock pot.

It was also the time when David was still commuting to Orlando—leaving on Monday morning and returning Thursday evening. I have to say that I was not tempted to stray. No one was half as interesting as my own spouse but phone bills were scary.

Back then everyplace was long distance from Cedar Key: doctors, dentists, friends. In the days before the Chiefland Wal-Mart, we were all "Sixty Miles from a Lot of Things."

The Cast of Characters in the beginning included our son Steven who was a senior at Cedar Key High School. Next-door neighbors to our rental with the picket fence were Judy and Larry. They had at least one cat and quite a few birds. Down the street was Mr. Brooks Campbell who invented an arthritis cure and had been written up in *National Geographic* as the Cedar Key lighthouse man. The cast of those first months included the school principal, Ms. Wells, and the other senior boys, Lamar, Jimmy and Jerald. I met our banker, Mr. Sidney, and within the first month, Ms. Janet Betts and Ms. Dorothy Tyson from the Historical Society. These would be my first friends. Mr. Kenny Edmunds had been talking to us about our house building ideas. He would be a messenger not to be forgotten—two days after moving to Cedar Key.

The cast continued to grow after those first months. There was Owen the Pelican Man, and Harriet Smith, the Bird Lady, who taught me about bird lice first hand; Richard Zeigler, the owner of a gas station in town; Polly Pillsbury, artist and founding mother of the Historical Society; Annette Haven, queen of the Garden Club; and so many others.

Many of the cast are gone now, either ashes-to-ashes or just gone away. I know some of their stories. Come waltz with me through the Wednesdays of Time when nothing ever happened in Cedar Key. No restaurants were open before evening. Cats and dogs lolled about on a summer day in the street. Storefronts said "Gone Fishin'" and meant it. Stroll through the brambles and briars of my thoughts. Take my hand and I'll guide you through some stormy days on the Island.

III
Cedar Key Then and Now

When asked how things have changed in Cedar Key since I first arrived, there is a tendency to say that nothing has really changed. Cedar Key is still the way it always was, the way Florida used to be. And then I close my eyes and in my mind wander up and down the streets, looking at the people I meet, the buildings, the businesses, the school—and then realize that the Cedar Key of today is less primitive, less innocent.

Then as now Cedar Key offered lots of places to eat: Frog's Landing, The Captain's Table, Johnson's Brown Pelican Restaurant, Helen's Place, The Seabreeze on Dock Street; Janice Coupe's The Heron Restaurant, The L&M Bar, The Cedars Lounge, Cedar Cove, The Island Hotel, Cook's Cafe (owned by a couple named Cook), all on 2nd Street; Rains Restaurant and The Other Place (later Salty's Oyster Bar). Most are now gone in one way or the other.

The banks then are still in the same places today but they too have different names. Today's Drummond Community Bank on 2nd Street was then a branch of Barnett Bank, perhaps the smallest branch of the chain. (Cedar Key State Bank started here in 1912.) This was our bank and Sidney Padgett our banker. There was no ATM and I regularly exercised my handwriting on checks (but left the account balancing to Dave).

Small satellite dishes (the unheard of wonders) had not yet arrived (the first, Primestar, would not be created until 1991). Over-the-air television was limited to the Gainesville channels, over sixty miles away. There were several possibilities for renting video tapes. We mostly rented at the Jiffy Store, and there were two more sources on Highway 24. One could rent tapes in plain brown wrappers. One rental store was a government creation as part of the then infamous Operation Fishhook sting of the early 1990's.

The Cedar Key Historical Society Museum was housed on the ground floor of the Gertrude Teas Building at the corner of Highway 24 and 2nd Street, where it is today. Upstairs was the law office of Al Simmons and David White. Behind the Museum was the Strong House, the historic home of a black Levy County family; the structure had been moved to the site from elsewhere in the county. The Andrews House, now behind the original museum building, was later acquired by the Historical Society and moved from its location at the end of 2nd Street, replacing the Strong House. The Museum became David's second career; he acted as Treasurer for many years. The Museum admission was one dollar.

The Cedar Key Library location was then in a state of flux. City Hall was to be expanded to include the library and pending completion of the space, the books themselves were stored in the Strong House. Today the library, which moved twice since that time, occupies what was then the fire house. The Friends of the Library was formed about this time and I was President for a while. (Dave and I joke that the risk of joining a local organization is that within two weeks you will be asked to be President.)

The Cedar Key Garden Club was very active back then, winning lots of awards from the State Garden Club organization. Some of the projects are still operational today: the recycling program, the trash bins, Adopt-A-Highway, trees planted in City Park.

Cedar Key School was the glue of the community. The school, no longer having a football team, concentrated on basketball, boys' and girls' teams, with success. The school's main building of this last decade of the 20th Century is not visible today. It, like it's predecessor, died by fire. The building we see today is reminiscent of that of seventy-five years ago, thanks in part to a campaign by the *Beacon*.

In 1988, the Cedar Key Lions Club was close to dream fulfillment–construction of a new clubhouse—when archaeologists from the University of Florida discovered human bones in the midden at the building site.

With the following year came the fight for the soul of Atsena Otie, armed policemen at city council meetings, and the disappearance at sea of local fisherman and city councilman Lud Johnson. That year also found me for brief moments Acting (and reluctant) Editor of the *Cedar Key Beacon*.

The early 1990's brought for Dave and me dreams of trails and mountains and backpacks. For Cedar Key, these years brought Project Ocean for the farm-raising of clams, a new wastewater treatment system, and the conviction of a then mayor and still city commissioner of battery in a bar room battle. The State of Florida denied the application for an underwater electric cable to Atsena Otie. This effectively stopped commercial and residential development on that island. The process began for the State to acquire the island. Owen the Pelican Man was at the center of controversy, and the Rosewood Incident was a much "cussed and discussed" subject. The State Marine Lab, on the verge of elimination from the budget, was saved at the last minute. For a brief while Cedar Key had two water towers, old and new, side by side.

And then came 1993's "Storm of the Century."

In looking back it occurs to me that an apt icon for the then Cedar Key, no longer with us, is that old, somewhat-rusted water tower, symbol of the Cedar Key that was.

IV
A Little More About Us

Somebody once told me that first God created the world—then he improved the plan and made Cedar Key, Florida. This place, with all its quirks, is my favorite place in the world. But then most of you know that the fast lane of State Road 24 is about all I can handle. Bright lights and big signs aren't my thing. Malls send me into a frenzy. My speed is more the deli counter at The Market. My feathers get ruffled by the sound of the aluminum cans going into the recycling bins.

If you haven't experienced it, cross the Number 4 Bridge at sunset. Look over to your right: there will be purples and pinks and oranges and a brilliant red ball that we take for granted. If the tide is low you'll see bared oyster bars and mudflats with tiny rivers snaking through the mud like spiderwebs. There will be unidentified birds wading and pecking and doing the things that birds do. Overhead the sounds of the larger birds will flap-flap-flap going home to roost. If the tide is high it will look like a tropical paradise. That red sun will paint the water like no artist could even imagine. The colors are on no palette except God's.

I turn into my little corner of the world content to leave the rest of the world to the east of me. Is this what the man meant when he said "East of Eden?"

My love affair with the island began sometime around 1960. It is the case with many University of Florida students, even to this day. We'd haul ourselves out of Gainesville given any opportunity at all. My roommate had a car: a little green Studebaker—the one that looked like it should have had an airplane propeller on its nose. She'd gas the baby up and we'd grab a book or two and head for Cedar Key. It seemed like it took forever to get here. We crossed that old wooden bridge into a time and place where there were no people—just birds and water, and the smells of fish, and grasses. We didn't venture too far. We just plopped ourselves at the end of what I now know as D Street—where the Gulfside Motel stands now. The row houses on First Street were not occupied and neither did the faucets have handles. We found no place to get a drink of water or even a bottled Coke. There was no market, no Jiffy Store.

In this place there was the Island Hotel. I was well underage and had no money or inclination toward anything except Coca-Cola but the only place to buy a cold beverage of any kind was in the bar of the hotel. Fifty cents! Ye Gads! Roommate Suzanne and I learned our lesson and brought water with us the next time! We were both fairly serious students. I had a paper to write this particular weekend. It was years before laptops. I brought my index card notes and portable typewriter with me and sat in the sand—how I wish I could remember what inanity I was composing. A gust of wind picked up my stacked file cards and whirlygigged the finished typed pages together and sent them spinning toward the water—into the water. I dived, retrieved some. Suzanne and I didn't come back to do too much work in Cedar Key after that. Later, I talked my new friend, David, into coming over with me for a Sunday afternoon. It wouldn't be the last Sunday we spent together on the island.

In the mid-1980's our goal was to move away from Orlando and still be able to put food on the table. Dave and I had discovered the romance of this group of islands years before and had not forgotten its charm and siren song. We were still smitten.

Buffeted by a then recent (1985) hurricane, Cedar Key had a bad reputation for storms and had reached the national media this way. There was no industry other than fishing and an emerging but low-key tourist trade.

In December, 1986 we purchased one of ten remaining lots on Boogie Ridge just outside the city limits of Cedar Key. This area is geographically and "properly" known as Haven's Island, split down the middle by State Road 24. The eastern side—called Osprey Point by some—took on the name Boogie Ridge from a juke joint nearby. (Or was that a man called Booger?) Believe what you will. We did all the things that would-be builders do: we ribboned the trees and picnicked on the lot. We brought our parents and our children to wade through the cactus with us and gloried at our marvelous taste, good fortune and clairvoyance. We'd checked out high-water marks from the 1985 hurricane; made sure we could get insurance. We planted seven more trees and a garden, complete with a scarecrow. The robins immediately ate the garden seeds and the heavy equipment would later squash the baby trees. We partook of an island Decemberfest and a Civil War re-enactment (directly across the Number 4 Channel from our new property).

We'd shown my dad the first rough drafts of the house we would build: "I'll have to build you an elevator!" My dad did indeed build elevators! He wouldn't build this one and he wouldn't see our house built and he wouldn't ever again visit with us on our island. We didn't know that then (so much for clairvoyance). My mother implored me to save the "beautiful cactus." As much as she liked to barefoot it around a yard, I couldn't believe she meant that. Still, I couldn't help but save some cactus.

By December, 1987 we had more than rough drafts of the house drawn up professionally, but not a board had been purchased nor a telephone pole set in the ground. We'd been negotiating with several builders, all of whom agreed that the house would either be a dream or a nightmare to build, fantasy or fiasco. It was one of the above.

Son Steven and I had moved to Cedar Key from Orlando in August 1987, two days before school started, leaving husband Dave behind to support our new lifestyle. Steve would begin his final year of high school knowing no one—in a class of four seniors (all boys). Our first residence, rented on the spur of the moment just to have shelter, was a single-wide mobile home on an unshaded, weedy lot on Gulf Avenue. While our minds and bodies were acclimating to Cedar Key Time and her people, our clothes and our toys were still in Orlando. I researched cultivating a hybrid sandspur that smelled like a rose. We grilled food on our little deck to keep the trailer cool and dragged chairs out to sit on the stoop in the evening. It was not a time of sadness. Steve and I felt more like conspirators: mystery people, aliens. No one knew whether we were on the lam, CIA agents or just running away from home. Better than that, no one seemed to want to know. We had no visitors, no phone and no solicitors. Junk mail still came to our Orlando address. A select few people knew our post office box number and I told them we lived in it, not far from the truth. For a brief time I recaptured the feeling of an eight-year-old on the last day of school: oblivious and unfettered. Could we make this work?

Was this arrangement our folly? That we were lonesome is undeniable. Steven was separated from his brothers and friends and for a time I had not even a familiar newspaper or telephone. My dad died three days after we moved to Cedar Key and Steve was left to manage on his own—cooking on a waffle iron—and going to a still strange school while I took an emergency flight to Utah. We had moved in a hurry to get Steve into school on time and had yet to establish a bank account. I left him with nineteen dollars cash in an alien world, with no transportation other than a bike and feet, and no communication means other than a book of stamps and a handful of quarters for the pay phone at the Jiffy Store a mile away.

That was when I first took those charges of "irresponsibility" seriously. Was this going to be a serious mistake?

Steve became immersed in schoolwork: projects and experiments. We dolled up the trailer with new curtains and a few of my appliances. We'd planned on being there as long as it took to sell the house in Orlando, when we'd be faced with gobs of furniture. Surprise! We'd made the young Doc and his wife (our prospective home buyers) an "offer they couldn't refuse." Within a week we rented a pleasant house at the end of Whiddon Avenue. We'd be in a real house (albeit still a rental): a pool, my own cat, and neighbors. I'd have a telephone and a yard with grass and a white picket fence.

If I didn't expect or want a block-party atmosphere at our new rental, I wasn't disappointed, but Larry and Judy were friendly neighbors. It was, however, our cats that broke the ice. A knee-high wall separated our properties and these two old tomcats sprawled on the blocks together, saying old man things like "Mrrrrl" and "Check out the Chicks in those Trees! Bird legs, but nice breasts." Shadow and Leonard would have this morning tête-à-tête, then stroll around looking important together. Judy was a bird fancier as well, raising cockatiels on her porch. They had a gruff big dog that we soon learned was all bluster and wagging tail. It was Larry, however, who knew everything and everybody and was quick to pass along the fruits of the Cedar Key Grapevine. For better or worse, I was learning about my adopted city.

All of our possessions were moved (even the cat)—with one major exception: Dad. Dave became the mysterious stranger who appeared on weekends and left in the wee hours on Monday morning before dawn. There is a bit of humor that emerged these first few weeks. Dave was having car problems and would show up in a different car each Thursday night. Then, of course, there was this middle-aged lady (me) who lived with an 18-year-old during the week. What a way to start life in a small town.

With two sons in college and one on the way, it was inconceivable that Dave could retire just yet. There was no way I could support the family on my sporadic nursing and writing career. Neither was it reasonable, with twenty-five years in a very specialized field of law, for Dave to set up practice in a small town where his reputation was unknown—even if there were the clients available. This was going to be tricky, and this is how I came to be affectionately known as a "commuter widow."

Complications securing permits and insurance due to the recent hurricane scare delayed building our new home. We began wondering when if ever we would move from the cute little rental house on Whiddon. The Orlando "mansion" was sold. We were committed. Included in the house plans was an office for Dave to do his work from home. His practice involved a great deal of paperwork. He was certain that the plan was workable with computer hookups, fax machines and telephones. Unfortunately, his firm didn't share his optimism. Dave continued to commute and be away four days of the week.

A curious thing started happening after a few months. Our own lifestyles began to change—individually. We found ourselves, married over twenty-five years, no longer a team. He took up aerobics at an athletic club in Orlando and I found I hated aerobic exercise anyplace. I started writing regularly for the newspaper and my columns both embarrassed and bored him. When I'd cook, he wasn't hungry. He'd want to socialize on Friday and Saturday mornings at the post office when I'd want to laze around the house after writing well into the wee hours. Were we growing independent or apart?

Steve made the track team and basketball teams. We became "boosters" and met school folks together on Friday night. With our other sons, Dave rarely attended games or meets. But this was Cedar Key–a world apart. Everybody does everything here. Suddenly I found him coming home early to attend Historical Society meetings, church covered-dish suppers, allowing himself to be volunteered to make clam fritters on a Festival Weekend with the senior class and act as chaperone for the boys with me on their senior trip to Gatlinburg, Tennessee. We delivered Woman's Club spaghetti suppers twice a year to shut-ins. He hauled trees for the Garden Club plant sales and participated in civic club yard sales. He assisted with helping develop the city Comprehensive Plan. He sold books at the Friends of the Library sale and toted plywood for tables across town on his shoulders. Rather, I should say he and I did these things together in the three days we would spend under the same roof. Some people might call this "quality time." I call it nice.

This village—and its unique quality—was the tie that binds.

The commuting years took a toll on Dave's vehicle. The Jeep Cherokee took down a deer on one of his after-dark runs home: it did nothing for its appearance. We stopped counting the water-pumps he had to purchase at out-of-the-way stations going or coming. The miles and gas mileage were grueling.

Our new house on Boogie Ridge was finally finished and we moved in. Dave had his "office" and the Case of the Commuter Widow was gradually solved. Dave cut back on his Orlando work-week. This did not help the car any and though he was in the house, I saw him no more than before: his workday started at 6 AM and he knocked off at 3 PM. It didn't bother me a lot that he ensconced himself in the "office" at 6 AM. I learned that independence is not being lonely and apartness is not being neglected. Our days together–after we got the rounds done downtown (together)—we might take the canoe out, be brave with the sailboat, re-plant the garden or pickle some green tomatoes. He might try to teach me a new function on the computer or print a picture or two for my articles.

This then was the background during my newspaper column-writing days, letting you the reader perhaps read between the lines of musings. As you read along, names of strangers may appear without further explanation; they were not strangers to my readers at the time; ask old timers around here if they remember them. And occasionally I refer to what would become our "Great Adventure," otherwise known as "The Trail, "The AT," "The Appalachian Trail," which in 1992 took us away from our island home to the mountains of the Eastern United States and a trek from Georgia to Maine.

Tuesday September 29th, 1987

Dear Grandma and Grandpa Roquemore,

Steve and I had a very uneventful (*Deo Gratis*) trip back to Cedar Key Sunday and stayed ahead of the rain all of the. way. I was extremely grateful for that since the car was so loaded and I had to rely on those outside mirrors. I do not like driving in the rain under any circumstances. Seems like the trip gets shorter each time. Maybe its because I don't get lost as much as I used to.

Today is a very quiet day—we cannot move into our new place until Thursday so my heart is not into packing any more stuff right now. The carload of things that I brought up are stacked in the bedroom awaiting transfer. It is amazing how much this little place will hold. Dave should be up Friday—pulling Davy's utility trailer with a couple of beds and whatever else he can manage to pack in. So you know what we will be doing this weekend. I think I'm beginning to feel like a transient. It is much easier though with just a backpack.

You might call this the beginning of a new era for all of us. It is exciting, scary and nostalgic. I don't mind leaving Waterwitch because I feel certain that I've turned it over to a loving family who have the energy and enthusiasm to care about that crazy house. It is certainly the most beautiful place in Orlando. Dave and I talked about it so much—we weighed the potential selling price against what these people could afford. We decided that you couldn't put a price tag on "joy," theirs and ours. I can see those precious little girls with their Halloween parties and their Christmas trees. I can also see Annalese scrubbing brass and tile and pulling down cobwebs until she is nuts. In a matter of days it will be theirs—and while I am nostalgic, I am not sad.

Now I guess I'd better get down to the reality of defrosting the refrigerator. I've written to Dave about the situation here motel-wise on the weekend of the Seafood Festival. We will work something out but it looks like Cedar Key is all booked. (I went everywhere yesterday.) See what he has to say. By that time we may have furniture and a sleeper as well.

Love,
Susannah

Monday February 27th 1989

Dear family,

Mondays are sort of weird around here. Dave leaves about five and I usually get up shortly after he goes. You might even call me "efficient" if you didn't know me so well. It's now seven and the dishes done, laundry going, cats fed and two articles written. I'll probably be late for the yoga class.

We've all been well throughout this cold weather. Jim had the flu but is over it. Steve, I think had a touch of homesickness but a dose of Southern Bell cured that.

I do love the yoga class. Some of the ladies are well into their seventies and you would be amazed at their suppleness. We have a lot of fun—I know that I've learned to trip over my feet in four different languages. Lesley (the instructor) keeps us literally "on our toes" and has been attempting to incorporate dance steps into the routines. Since I was born with two left feet and two right arms I can never get the four limbs going the right way at the right time. One cannot be proud and take this class.

Yesterday we went to Sharkey's and Connie's 45th wedding anniversary open house. He is the vicar of the Episcopal Church and they are just super people. Connie had just had foot surgery (bunions) and was in a cast and on crutches. They live in a cute little house behind the church and had the party there rather than at the parsonage. The same people attend the same parties and one of these days Dave and I will start getting the names straight. Dave gets amused that everyone knows us—how could they help with my picture in the paper once a week—of course they know him by reputation. He blushes nicely. I'm enjoying the writing and hope I don't embarrass anyone too much. I never know what article is going to come out at any given time since I write them in bunches and put them in the box.

Next weekend we have two more parties to attend: Ruth Wagner will be ninety—she virtually opened the museum ten years ago—at age 80—and has been chief cook and bottle washer for it ever since. We are taking her to the Heron for a luncheon (we being the Historical Society). Then another open house-dinner buffet. Cedar Key is very lively this time of year—soon the winter people will have their grand exodus—meanwhile it can get rather hectic.

The art festival is April 15-16th and I have scoured the town for a room—there is a possibility, but slim, of a cancellation. What happens is that most of the nice places are really condos—and the owners come in for the festival. There are very few real rentals. I know one lady and her husband who have a condo at Island Place—that's the one we showed you with the little utility area, bunks, etc.—they are leaving town before the festival! Don't know if she has it already signed up or not. I will ask. Otherwise, why don't you all just plan to spend the night with us??? I know it wouldn't be as convenient as having a place of your own or a bed of your own but we promise not to let the cats invade your territory. I'll put a fresh roll of toilet tissue in the bathroom and find a clean towel or two. If Dave is feeling magnanimous he will even put the coffee pot on the timer so you can have a fresh brew when you awaken (we've been taking lessons in hostmanship).

Please don't worry about the boys. If they come in—Steven might—and David, who knows? They are quite used to a mattress. That is about the best I can do for the time being. Suffice it to say that we'd love having you.

Dave said that you were thinking of getting a condo here. I agree with Dave that if you do indeed sell Lake Placid, it would be a lovely idea. Last fall they were running about 80k at Park Place. I know this because Janet Betts thought that was what I was looking for for Mama. Of course it wasn't, but she brought me literature on several available units. There is a move afoot to build a really spectacular condo—not a high-rise—but in keeping with the historical nature and style of Cedar Key—down at the end of the street beyond Park Place. It would be part of the preservation-conservation movement. The land hasn't even been purchased yet—it is still in the gossip stages. The land is owned by my doctor—who lives in Gainesville now. His family started the fiber factory here at the turn of the century. He still has a residence here. He has vowed not to spoil the views, etc. I hope I can trust him.

The weekends are just too short. Dave's garden is coming along fairly well despite the cold weather set-back. He ate his first radishes. Today is warm and I shall take all the houseplants back outside. We have a new lemon tree still in its pot. We planted a persimmon, a tangerine and a Satsuma orange that I hope survived. He has put in lettuces, chard, beets, radishes, carrots, mustard. I've ordered garlic bulbs, asparagus, onion sets, daylilies, and a pile of other stuff from catalogs. Catalog shopping is one of my greater vices. Oh yes—three thornless blackberry bushes. Dave promises to build me an arbor so we can grow grapes and take me to Newberry to select some blueberry bushes. We've transplanted two cedar trees and three pines–two of which look healthy. In this terrible soil one never knows. The driveway is about halfway done. Mac doesn't work fast. He told me, "Maybe Thanksgiving." Unfortunately , he didn't tell me which Thanksgiving.

Must go and put on my dancing clothes. Much love to you and your grandson who doesn't know how to write a letter.

Susannah

Tuesday afternoon

Dear Orlando Family,

Spring has indeed sprung. And I'm smitten with a case of Spring Fever—generally translated: I don't want to do anything that sounds like work! (So what else is new?)

The driveway workers were here this morning after a three-week hiatus. At this rate I may have a driveway by Christmas—which year? It is turning out very pretty and park-like. They bulldozed the mountain of dirt and removed the trash so it is almost respectable. Dave and I must build up that soil so it supports life before planting any ground cover or flowers. Everybody expects us to put azaleas in there but Dave is on a native-plant kick and so far we haven't found anything that loves shade and sand at the same time. He brought up about ten large bags of leaves last weekend and we are about to start our compost heap. Our trees are shedding as well. So maybe it is not as futile as it looks! What we need is a cow (instant fertilizer). His garden is looking good finally, the lettuces are of edible size and the tomatoes are blooming. We have about six types of peppers, chard, onions, and a big strawberry patch. My herbs are thriving and I keep finding new ways to use them. Dilled and basiled eggs? Fenneled spaghetti sauce? Some pretty creative endeavors! My parsley bolted and it is very pretty although I doubt it is tasty anymore. Steve has a huge pot of parsley that he keeps in his room to munch on. My children are almost as weird as their parents. I've ordered three thornless blackberry bushes. The wild ones are like a briar patch—blooming and making berries. The birds love them!

This past weekend I tried to haul all of the rocks from the driveway construction to build a lily-bed border. No amount of yoga prepared me for hauling rocks. We planted another cedar tree; actually, a friend pulled it up from the woods and gave it to me.

Last week I was inducted into the Cedar Key Woman's Club. I guess that means that I am an old timer. Most of them are, actually. I like the people who sponsored me. But there are many that I know only by name. I think I will enjoy the association but I do have to be careful not to get in over my head. Everything sounds so interesting! Dave and I have joined Friends of the Library. That involves only donating books and manning a book sale once in awhile. Do you have books/magazines that you want to get rid of? They are in desperate need. Cedar Key is renovating old City Hall and the library will get larger quarters once it is done. Thanks to Dave, Cedar Key has a fairly recent set of Florida Statutes.

We recycle our magazines thru it. Last year I wound up buying back a book that I'd inadvertently donated (my camera manual). It does get a little funky around here.

I just got back from a luncheon feting our yoga teacher. She did these classes gratis but we took up a collection and bought her a lovely turquoise necklace and earrings to remember us by. She wears lots of good but chunky jewelry. Not my style at all but very nice. She is a very pretty lady—chic. Seventeen of us went–it was almost like a going away party for half of Cedar Key.

The seasonal people will be exiting next month and I will definitely miss them. The social season is winding down.

I guess Dave told you that he is now Treasurer of the Historical Society. I did not nominate him, either. I'm on the Board but wouldn't even inform him of the nomination. I think that he is delighted, but it is not really an easy job either. Especially since he isn't here all the time. I deliver checks—Dave is a stickler for legalities (makes sense) and most groups somehow sidestep some of the details along the way. He is now trying to learn the routine. Dave is one of the darlings of the Society and has to keep the peace. He is genuinely fond of the people he's associated with here. Almost all of us are somewhat eccentric.

Janet and Bill Betts want us to go golfing with them in Chiefland some day. There is a nice club there—reminds me of the Lake Placid course and club and the dues are manageable for the entire family. Dave found his clubs but we have no idea whatever happened to the ones I used to use.

Well, I have a new editor at the Beacon. Julie sold the Paper to "Salty." You might remember he owned the restaurant now called "The Other Place." He left Cedar Key just about the time we came—moved to Orlando—he came back. I found out from Julie that he likes my column (which I guess should make me feel good) so I guess I won't get fired this week at least. Maybe he will give me a raise? (That is supposed to be a joke.) All I would have to do is make some money and mess up David's carefully organized tax returns! I might have to leave the country!

I hope you all are well. Except for the oak blossoms and the rock hauling, I think I'll make it.

The paper has run out and I have run out of inspiration.

Love to you,
Susannah

Mother "Touched" by Ceremony

Dear Editor,

My family moved to Cedar Key last year, enrolling our youngest son in Cedar Key High School in his senior year. This could have been what psychologists would call "traumatic."

The graciousness, warmth and caring atmosphere of the school dispelled all of my fears, and most of Steven's. The teachers and students welcomed Steve and me into the community and made us feel at home.

For those of you who missed the graduation ceremony, I can only say you missed touching the pulse of Cedar Key. I usually do not cry at ceremonies: weddings, funerals or graduations—but this was so very special. Sons presented moms with bouquets; sweet and gentle jibes at classmates; and eloquent speakers reminding the graduates of their responsibilities to the world.

To my son's principal, Mrs. Wells and her wonderful colleagues and faculty my roses go.

Those of us who love Cedar Key don't care if we have four, five or fifty graduates. The fact that those students receive this quality is very important.

For this I thank you and shed tears for the others that are not so blessed.

Susan Roquemore, Cedar Key

A Story Never Told

Our son Steven was a transfer student from Orlando Boone High School for the school term 1987-88. He would be in his senior year. You might think that this would be a terrible trauma for a young man of that age. In reality, Steve was agreeable. "Just don't switch me in the middle of the year." That meant we'd be moving before the school year started. What none of us realized was that Levy County schools started two weeks before those in Orange County. It has something to do with the watermelon harvests—as if Cedar Key has a lot of watermelon growers. We thanked realtor Carmen Proctor when she found the only vacancy in town that August weekend. Carmen sent someone out the next day with a flit gun to kill the fleas. It was going to be a difficult transition. We just didn't know how difficult.

David left us on Sunday to get back to work for Monday morning. Steve would start school Monday morning. I'd try to make sense of this trailer living. We'd brought only a few things with us. For a time, we'd be commuting almost as much as Dave would be. We were trying to fix up our house in Orlando for sale. We'd been taken by surprise by this early school opening. Still, a promise is a promise.

It was Monday night I think—maybe it was Tuesday—when

Steve and I had retired. In this place the bedrooms were at opposite ends of the box-car and we'd already switched belongings twice. This was a grand adventure. He had his girlie pictures in place and I was missing our cat. We'd both conked out when a sudden rapping, tapping at the chamber door. It was really more like banging. I said "Steve. Get the Door!" I didn't know anyone (I thought) in town and was nervous. He did. It was Kenny Edmunds, a fellow we'd talked to about building a house. He jumped back ten feet when I came to the door. It was like he expected me to be holding a shotgun. I wished I had been as I was still nervous about opening that door in the middle of the night to a stranger. Kenny was and is ever the gentleman and told me that Dave had called and I needed to call him right away.

These are the days before cell phones. Neither did we have a house phone since we'd been in residence only a day or so. "Steven, grab the money jar!" We both put shoes on and I think I had presence of mind to cover my nightgown with a trench coat. I think. We would drive the few blocks to the Jiffy Store at the corner of Whiddon and Highway 24 and camp at the pay phone. Middle of the night phone calls are always awful. Who died? I was in terror of just who that person might be.

Just before I left town I'd had a terrible confrontation with our oldest son who was in his best recalcitrant form. He was twenty-three years old and has a Taurean stubborn streak a mile wide. He was born with my Prussian temperament and none of my age. He drove a souped-up car and frankly, I was scared he was in a ditch someplace. He wasn't. Anything after that was a relief. You have to be a mother of sons to understand. When David told me that my dad died in Utah, I was sad. Very sad. Few people understand why I didn't cry.

Steve and I fed dimes and quarters into the phone while I called my brother and sister-in-law in Utah where Mama and Daddy were visiting. Dave arranged a plane flight out of Tampa at 3 PM. It was now about 3 AM. I took a bath, washed my hair. I tossed some clothes into a bag. Never in my wildest imagination would I have expected to be traveling across country. Surprising myself, we did have a suitcase. As dawn came, I gave Steve instructions (trust me, I can be more dictatorial than Stalin ever thought about being): "Under no circumstances are you to try to use this gas stove. It hasn't been checked out and I don't want you blown up! Cook everything on the waffle iron." I said that—and I meant it. I couldn't give him a credit card as I had to have it with me. I had exactly nineteen dollars in my purse and he had the penny jar. Dave couldn't come up and get him until Friday and I had to take the car to get to the airport in Tampa. Steve, a pretty shy person, was left totally alone in a miserable house in a school where he knew no one, in a town where he knew no one—with no phone. The radio received WKTK and that was it. To make matters almost unreal, he would spend his eighteenth birthday—a day or two away—here, like this.

Part Two

On Newspapers & Writing

Susan deep into the keyboard

New Weekly Newspaper Debuts

The *Cedar Key Beacon* debuted today (Thursday) as the island's first locally owned and operated weekly newspaper also serving southwest Levy County. Owners and publishers of the newspaper as Beacon Publishing, are Julie Stetzel and Carla Anderson, with offices on D Street in Cedar Key. . . . The *Beacon* is a newspaper designed to serve Cedar Key and surrounding communities with local news and features each week on a subscription basis.

The Cedar Key Beacon, September 9, 1984

Beacon To Become a "Mom & Pop" Operation!!

Ms. Ruby O'Steen Clayton of Delray Beach has announced the engagement and up-coming wedding of her daughter, Robin "Sue" Clayton Heillman to Michael J. Raftis, both of Cedar Key. . . . She is currently employed as the Managing Editor of the *Cedar Key Beacon*. . . . He is currently employed as a Marketing Consultant and president of Advertising Design, Inc. and Publisher of the *Cedar Key Beacon*.

The wedding will take place Saturday, October 14th at 2 PM at the Cedar Key Episcopal Church followed by a reception at Cedar Cove.

The Cedar Key Beacon

According to an article published in the Orlando (Florida) Sentinel, Robin Heillman first met Mike Raftis at the Cedar Key Market's fresh meat counter. He had recently purchased the Cedar Key Beacon. She asked if she could put a "personal ad" in the paper since she had not had a date in eighteen months. Instead, he asked her out; and not long after, hired her as editor.

At Home in the Fourth Estate

The "estate" was then located at the corner of 2nd and D Streets, heralded by a simple sign: "The Cedar Key Beacon." I'd been reading the paper regularly at the newsstand price of twenty-five cents. I could have bought a *Wall Street Journal* for that price but it was rare that the *Journal* carried local Cedar Key news or the name of our latest chief of police.

I knew one of the columnists, Harriet (the "Bird Lady"), who taught me to hold a pelican without getting seriously wounded. She didn't teach me how to keep from getting covered in bird mites, but I respected Harriet's musings about things wild and critters local. I didn't have much to qualify me as a journalist other than the fact that I'd been late to my own college graduation and had been seated with the journalism and advertising college.

I owned and could use a typewriter and if there was one thing I loved—really loved—to do, it was write. I never expected to get answers to my letters: no one ever had time in this life to get as far as the signature. It never even occurred to me that I could write for a real newspaper. In the movies, it all looked like bedlam and editors were holy people who weren't disturbed. My high school and college experience did nothing to boost my confidence: it was just too easy—thus, it couldn't be work; ergo the *Florida Alligator* and high school *Cor* didn't count.

My sense of work ethic is a bit perverse. Work is worthwhile only if one is miserable. When it stops being fun, I stop doing it. Therefore I do everything in my power to avoid work. When I paint a room, I dress in a hair shirt. I hate painting! Wallpapering is fun, therefore not work. I'm much more tired after painting a baseboard than I am hanging a room of paper. I could lose myself in the printed page, especially if I had created that page.

I never consciously said "I'm going to write a column." It just happened. I'd more or less sneak downtown and push copy under the door of the *Beacon* office when I was sure no one was there. The copy was usually letter-perfect, typed and double-spaced, at least in the early days. One day I was horrified to be discovered: "Hi, I'm Robin! I want to take your picture!" Ye Gads and Holy Catfish, who is Robin? I hadn't even noticed that the editors had changed. That sick picture ran above my column in the *Beacon* for several years.

Meeting deadlines and coming up with ideas for a folksy column once a week was no problem. I had more words and thoughts than I had good sense. At first I wrote with the sense of the ridiculous. I became increasingly aware that life was crazy enough without exaggerating. Erma Bombeck had used this device to get laughs and while I bowed to her humor, I didn't need it. I didn't need to suggest that the laundry had been on pre-soak for thirteen years or that my children cleaned their rooms only when the mold started walking around fighting back.

Inky Veins Inspires Writer
January 1989

It is a real pleasure to be writing for the *Beacon* but I will admit that this is not my first venture into the world of journalism.

I did in fact graduate with the College of Advertising and Journalism students at the University of Florida without taking one course in that department. I had the only apricot tassel on my mortarboard, in a sea of black-and-whites.

OK, I'll confess. I was late to graduation and had to be sneaked into the hall. I found myself sitting next to an old flame who appropriately stage whispered: "What are *you* doing here?" I asked him the same question in return.

In my early undergraduate days, I used to hang around with the journalism crowd. They were the ones who stayed up all night in the basement of the old Florida Union building drinking stale coffee in an effort to get out yet another issue of the *Florida Alligator* (pre-independent days).

It was not by chance that I found myself trying to help salvage the yearbook that promised not-to-be that year (the *Seminole* yearbook shared office space with the *Florida Alligator*). The editor (and good friend) had been suspended from school for driving an unauthorized vehicle on campus too many times and parking in the president's slot. He would give me paste-ups and I'd secretly put them in sometimes the right place.

At first I tried writing hard news—really hard-hitting articles—like coverage of homecoming floats and house decorations. It was only later that I discovered I could only make light of such rigors of college life.

This career really began when I was about four years old and my older brother, Tommy, decided that we needed a neighborhood newspaper. My other brother, Jack, and I were to be his investigative reporters.

My parents, by and large, went along with reporting such things as the rice that covered the ceiling in the Engle household ("The Pressure Cooker Incident"). Daddy drew the line when Jack reported the words he said to a flat tire! We had censorship even in those days. My parents never heard of the First Amendment. We must have published at least four issues before we ran out of carbon paper and went on to bigger things(!)—like a radio station.

In those days, kids entertained themselves with the most sophisticated equipment available, just like today. Tommy rigged up a loud speaker to the outside and we would use comic books as our script. I was Lois Lane on more than one occasion. The neighbors eventually pulled our radio station's license.

My brothers truly influenced my literary career. At the height of McCarthyism, Jack was the editor of his high school newspaper. On April 1 of his senior year, he authorized the printing of Hillborough High's *Red and Black* issue of *Pravda*. Jack's days as editor were threatened. Later he wrote scientific literature in every language but Russian. Tommy became the editor of the Emory University *Spoke,* which has been revived this year as a humor magazine after a forty-year hiatus.

Printer's ink is in my veins, probably literally. Daddy worked for the *Tampa Tribune* for twenty-five years and brought his work clothes home to be laundered (he was chief of maintenance). Unless you have experienced a press room of a large metropolitan newspaper of the fifties you won't understand the meaning of ink. He would sit me on those large rolls of paper that would become the Sunday funnies. The pressmen would make for me those little square paper hats that I later learned to entertain my children with by making for them.

While Daddy didn't believe half of what he read and little of what he heard, I grew to revere the written word, and respect those people who try to get the facts straight–and out on time.

Writing to my family was something a person did but never did for a living. (God forbid you didn't have a *real* job!). It was inconceivable to either of my parents that I might want to actually have a career writing things. They saw me as a nurse wearing a white uniform and a white cap with a black band, white shoes and stockings and puncturing people with long hypodermic needles. In truth, I saw myself that way too.

What none of us reckoned on was that the College of Nursing at the University of Florida was rhetoric driven. Under the tutelage of a master craftswoman and idealist, Dean Dorothy Smith, we student nurses wrote and wrote and wrote our way to degrees in nursing. She insisted that we be more than technicians. She insisted that we be educated, not trained like elephants or seals. She made each of us eloquent in our art. Why we did something was more important than how we did it (sometimes).

I was a better diagnostician and writer than I ever would be the craftsman. No one wanted to believe this, because I could really do some imaginative nursing (and still can). However, my heart was more in writing the report than it was in doing the work. Today, there are places for people like me in the nursing profession—but in those days, the new breed of college-educated nurse was not just a novelty, she (and there were few males) was resented, sneered at, given work she was ill prepared for and generally burned out before she got dry behind the ears. I took a twelve-year sabbatical from the profession. No love was lost but whatever I thought I knew I realized I had forgotten when I went back and jumped into the profession with both feet in 1980.

How did I get from there to here? It has to be obvious that during those child-oriented years when I was a stay-at-home mom (which is a modern term for "housewife"), I never stopped writing. I'd had some things published, for pay, but largely my writing was done on a volunteer basis for the many organizations that stay-at-home moms engage in. I didn't write to be funny but people would laugh. One friend kept all of my letters in a file cabinet. My mother would share my letters with cronies. I wore out typewriters. If I was sad, I'd write. When I was angry I'd write and then file the letters. When I was happy I'd write. That is how, and why, when I got to Cedar Key Florida—without a real friend within shouting distance—I started writing. And really—despite what a lot of people think—have never quit.

September Song

This is my most favorite thing and the first thing I ever wrote for the Beacon. I wrote it long ago when it was my first September in Cedar Key when the world was new. You didn't know me and I didn't know you. I wrote it as a tribute to being alone with only the joy of a son and the sun and the moon, and a man I loved to greet me sometime soon. (Soon, but when?) So, I wrote my thoughts, September thoughts, for the Beacon. Days have drifted into years. I smile when I recall my writing this song. They were not long days. We drifted along several Septembers. I remember them year-to-year and only fear that I might forget someday that joy that was yesterday.

There is a special time of year here in Cedar Key that cannot be held in the hand or touched. It must be inhaled and felt. It is September.

September is the threat of storm and beguiling breezes. It is humid afternoons and not knowing whether to open windows, turn air-conditioning off, or to sleep off the lazy afternoons under a tree in a hammock.

It is a time of spectacular sunrises over Waccasassa Bay and amazing starlit nights, the skies washed by an afternoon rain. It is goldenrod season, and coriopsis season, and the fields are ablaze with yellow flowers. The cicadas and frogs (toads?) sing because they have plentiful meals of mosquitoes.

The town itself is quiet. It has been said that one can fall asleep in the middle of Second Street and run the risk of being run over only by a Cedar Key stray cat.

Tourists have gone home to get children back in school after Labor Day. Some locals have deserted the island earlier to reach for cooler climes and will visit relatives until our own cool season settles in. It is a special time for those of us who choose to stay here during September.

Driving back from Bronson the other day this driver met not one car coming or going in thirty-five miles. Is that a measure of pleasure?

Cedar Key in September offers whistling winds through the pines and assorted cross-country track team members sweating their way around the streets after school. For the moms of school children, it means finding lunch money change and the inevitable trip to school at least once a week with a math or English book. It means seven o'clock alarms and making popcorn for the meet or game on Friday.

September is not always a kind month. We should forgive her because tonight's balmy breezes make up for all of her transgressions.

If we are to experience a world-class event, we should at least experience one September in Cedar Key. It will not be predictable. It may not even be enjoyable. It will, however, color your memory with indelible shades of pink, violet, orange and blue. Green and yellow. Reds, mauves. Walk down into our Fall sunset. Melt into the Gulf with the sun, but take the insect repellent. They like the sunsets, too—and they were here first.

You can walk what we call beaches and feel the splendor of September. It won't happen again until next year.

Cedar Key is not for everyone, but for September's Children, she is just right.

Dear Robin, Wish You Were Here
August 1989

In August 1989 Editor Robin Raftis occupied a hospital room for surgery and I temporarily occupied her chair as Editor of the Cedar Key Beacon, a proverbial "hot seat" if one ever existed.

If there is one thing I've learned this past week it is that there are scarier things than giving birth or capsizing in a canoe. It seems that I have made it a habit to get myself into situations that would stress out Mother Teresa! Once, I found myself director in charge of a computer camp in Vermont. First of all, everyone knew that I could zap a computer by entering a building with one in it! Whole video arcades would grow silent when I entered a mall.

Now I find myself sitting in Robin's chair working on the *Cedar Key Beacon*. Forgive me if I blather on about the fact that the paper actually got out last week. Robin had suggested that I not pour Coca-Cola into the word processor and that it did not respond to four-letter voice commands. Mr. Raftis walked me through the functions and sometimes wheeled me through them. Talented Marie was ever so patient when I kept losing things.

The *Beacon*, as I have known it (and know it better now), wants to report items of interest to both our local residents and our visitors alike. Sometimes, with my feature-writer slant, I tend to see humor even where there is none. No one is mad at me yet, but tomorrow is another day!

On second thought, there is one resident that has a pet peeve: I let his prize tomato plant wither all week.

If We Have Stepped on Any Toes
August 1989

In today's *Beacon*, on another page, I make mention of the fact that I hadn't made anyone mad at me yet. That was yesterday's news. You know, I've gone and done it and I don't feel bad about it at all.

In a policy statement that is printed every week on the "Letters" page the *Beacon* clearly says that it will not print any letter that contains "inflammatory, libelous or slanderous statements or are of a commercial nature." Sometimes we find that it is only a phrase that needs deleting but sometimes it is the whole letter!

The *Beacon* received such a letter this week directed to a private businessman and his business. It makes no difference whether the information is true—the tone of the letter defamed the man and impugned his character. The decision not to run this letter was based on the *Beacon*'s policy of fair play and responsibility. You don't have to advertise with us to get the same treatment.

Elected officials should expect the limelight. Still, the same policy holds. We will scrutinize your service to the public but your character is your own.

We welcome honest, angry letters; funny letters; sweet letters; letters of information and letters of indignation. We'll take the bouquets of sandspurs directed at us and plant them in print. It remains not only our right, but our obligation, not to enter into personal squabbles. We won't print anonymous letters, no matter how nice the sentiment.

We want, need and invite your input: news, features, stories. There are some pretty talented folks out there in Cedar Key Land and you are probably one of them. Come into the *Beacon* office and say hello or leave copy in the blue box. If you have pictures to share with the world, just make sure they are identified.

Until I sat in this seat I had no idea which or what articles or letters took precedence; how much room was in the paper for a given edition; and how it keeps changing from hour to hour. Patience is a virtue, but Prudence is an art. The *Beacon* is studying art. I've brought a package of band-aids to the office. I'm a Registered Nurse and know how to apply them to stepped-on toes.

Commentary
March 1991

Today

you might learn something that you never even considered before. Today you might begin to wonder why people even think about putting out newspapers. I can tell you first hand that it is not an easy thing to do, and I know Robin and Mike and Dave and Julie and those before them bit through lower lips many times.

Occasionally, there arrives an ugly letter which not only demeans what I am doing, but the efforts of my colleagues. There is a temptation to deep-six these letters. I do not believe in this approach. "Let the man have his say." The *Beacon* has been criticized for its typographical errors but rarely for its text. I do not hesitate to ask the critics to proof the *Wall Street Journal* or *New York Times* or even the *Gainesville Sun* for such common errors.

Let me tell you how it works. These are not family or trade secrets. Most of the columnists submit their stories on a weekly basis. Some use tapes, some computer disks. Some submit theirs in longhand, and others use manual typewriters. Some call the information in. Some are early, some are late. The *Beacon* could fire these people—but who would replace them? The *Cedar Key Beacon* is about and for the people of Cedar Key and its visitors, its organizations, its school, its churches. Who takes those pictures, and who develops and prints them? And who pays for the film, the chemicals and the paper? If this is beginning to sound like a sob story, it is not. Every one of us involved in getting the paper out on time with a mix of news and features enjoys the struggle. We don't have the most modern equipment available but we have the technology at hand and the expertise to use it. We don't have a stable of cub reporters or photographers. We don't have too many people who can subsist on slave wages for overtime into the wee hours.

This newspaper is an act of love for our town and if anyone suggests that people make money running anything except a Hearst operation, they've not been at the *Cedar Key Beacon* at 4 AM on a Thursday morning. The paper then must go to Chiefland to the printer. If the printer is not running late, it is back in the office about 10 AM to be labeled and taken to the post office by 11:30. News stand carriers take it to Bronson, Chiefland and points in between. Somebody else hauls it to Joe for local and distance mailing. Believe it or not, both go out on the same day! The *Beacon* mails to APO and FPO boxes, as well as to England, Canada, France, and the Philippines, which require special handling. More than 1,400 newspapers are handled within a period of an hour, on approximately four hours sleep, by maybe three people.

Long about midnight we start dropping apostrophes. I know I've been known to spell my own name wrong. Some of you readers forgive us. Some don't. It's a world-class act down at the *Beacon* office on Wednesdays. Salty pays his bills by working in Orlando three days a week. Robin gets paid sometimes. We think that the *Cedar Key Beacon* is worth it—that newspapering is worth it. Cedar Key is worth it. All of us ramble a bit. How much can we say about Desert Shield or Steve Spurrier that hasn't already been said? We won't cover for our neighbors—but neither will we crucify them. We welcome your stories, your gripes and your suggestions. We'll fix your typos—just please don't be mean to us when we do.

I've asked to write this commentary because I thought I could do it better than either Raftis. They couldn't tell you that they get downright hurt. They wouldn't say that. I don't mind saying it at all. Maybe newspaper people aren't supposed to get tired or drop apostrophes when the elbows get soggy. If I knew where to find a four-hundred-pound apostrophe, I know where I would place it.

Write Right!
September 1989

A few weeks ago, I was really on a writing binge. It must be akin to what runners feel after running full tilt—the endorphins are released and it is a natural high that is so very sweet and addictive. Sadly, the only thing I get from running is shin-splints and tired. But if the way I feel after writing a long letter is any indication, then I can understand.

Many times I don't even need an audience: the joy is in the doing. Writing is a beautiful communion of art and craft—and to some extent is a God-given talent. It is a talent that must be nurtured and can't be forced. It must be encouraged, since some of us have vivid stories to tell but have been intimidated by a well-meaning teacher or parent who stresses the *craft* more than the *art*.

How many times have we not heard the complaint: "The children never write!" or "No one sends Thank You's anymore." I have a pretty good idea why: Someone is going to sit there and say "Do you have *any* idea how that child spelled "congratulations?"— never taking into consideration it was the thought that counted.

My first experience with serious writing was in the third grade when my class was assigned the proverbial "What I Did On My Summer Vacation." (It had been a pretty exciting summer—we'd traveled as a family to Atlanta for a college graduation.) We picnicked on Stone Mountain back when the only thing that was there was a radio tower.

Mama suggested that I write about scrambling up the rocks with my fourteen- and twenty-one-year-old brothers. "Keep it simple and don't try to write about the whole summer." She suggested a title: "The Mountain and Me." I told her that was bad grammar! She said, "It's poetic license." Of course my teacher crossed out the "Me" and corrected it to "I." I was infuriated as only a seven-year-old writer could be: "My mom says that is poetic license and leave my title alone."

To be sure, the whole point of most writing is communication and we have to work within the confines of language. We can't all be Lewis Carrolls and create words and expect others to know what we mean or Tolkeins who create whole worlds. Reasonable punctuation and grammar are necessary at some point—but not when you are trying to instill a love of writing in a youngster. Just like with reading, the desire should come first and the mechanics later. There is *always* something to praise about a child's effort to write.

My son Steven has always had difficulty with language—due to some physical and perceptual problems identified only after he had begun school. Steven, however, has been a faithful correspondent wherever I happened to be—with some of the most charming and informative letters! Over the years, with much determination on his part and lots of patience from teachers and parents, he is finally learning grammar in writing. What could have turned out to be a stifled child and adult is turning into a creative writer only now learning the craft.

David the eldest writes with precision and feeling and force. He is a craftsman who is out to communicate ideas. Jimmy prefers the telephone. He doesn't find that *joie de vivre* in writing a letter. Short, sweet and to the point—"Send Money, Love, Jim!"

As with reading, writing is so much fun! And gives so much joy to others. The stationery can be the back of an envelope and the implement a stub of a pencil or a crayon. You don't need matching envelopes or felt tip pens. Your handwriting doesn't have to be Parker Penmanship.

Some of the very few rules I follow when I write a letter are:

- ☐ If you write in anger or sorrow, allow a three-day cooling off period, re-reading the letter and editing it. You may want to "deep-six" it.
- ☐ Be newsy but don't dwell on either tragedy or ailment or bragging unless this is a truly intimate letter.
- ☐ Don't forget to put a stamp on the envelope.

My favorite letter of all time came a few years ago when I was teaching in Vermont. It read in part: "Dear Mom: Guess I'd better tell you right out, the cat's gone! We think he is dead. Do you remember all that meat in the freezer? It is no more. We had a flood but nobody got really electrocuted. Dad's gone to Peru. Did you read what is happening in Peru? By the way, how do you get blood out of the living room rug? We had a tornado the night Dad left but he said not to worry, he'd get the tree off the roof when he got back. P.S. the cat came back. Dad hasn't"

Write a letter. Make someone's day a little brighter.

Since this article was written a whole new genre of writing has emerged. Computerese, aka facebooking, texting, twittering, has made the younger generation bold with the written word. Channels are open like never before. The question remains: Are communication skills better for the wide practice? Hmmm...

My Life as a Syntax Error
March 1990

A few years ago (1984), in one of my more febrile fits, I enrolled in a course that was listed in the college catalog as "Basic Computers." Here we had this dandy little machine that the kids all adored and that their father paid homage to on weekends and it, well, just sat there during the day. I wasn't into Dragon-Mania or Astro-Boys, and joy-sticks showed me just how uncoordinated I could be. It blinked its green screen at me friendly-like. Surely, I could be mistress of such a gadget.

I'd taken lots of basic courses: sewing, Chinese cooking, automobile maintenance. In each of these, the instructor started out with how to plug it in, how to chop a water chestnut or how to lift a hood. I was then taken aback when the instructor walked into the room.

Son Jimmy was sixteen and was teaching a youth soccer team. The instructor could have been one of his forwards. This had to be the "Doogie Howser" of computers. He started out by putting things on the blackboard. I copied them. Everybody else was nodding but I am thinking, "What the devil is he writing?" I looked around. These children should be dunking for apples, not in a college class. "Any questions?" the cute kid said. "Lots of them, starting with why am I here?"

I made some big mistakes that first day—like not dropping the course. I remember my parents' admonition: "Drop a course and the money stops." Never mind that Mama and Daddy had long since stopped paying for my education, and that David, who was, started out in engineering and wound up in law, but it was ingrained in me to stick it out.

One of our exercises was to inventory a library. A year of so later it occurred to me that the lady in the Library of Congress probably took the same course I did (and got the same grade).

Those of you who have heard me speak of the "dark days" of my marriage may rightfully understand that these were computer days. I'd learned that BASIC wasn't basic and none of it bore the slightest resemblance to English. Not even the manual was written in English. It was a cross between Esperante and Hieroglyphics and teen speak (GOSUB, GOTO, and a bunch of other GO's). In those days we had a very user-unfriendly program. In fact, it was so unfriendly that I sprinkled arsenic on the drive now and again. Once, when I had entered thirty pages of report into the thing, Florida Power decided to eat them. I cried. I did more than cry, I cursed.

It was quite a few years before I sat down behind a keyboard again. David came over and said something like: "Come here, I want to show you something." Sucker for a good-looking man that I am, I followed him. It was another computer! Another printer! Just what I always wanted!

That was several years ago. Now we argue over who gets to use it and when. He spends his weekends fixing what I break during the week. Baby has been on Disk Doctor all weekend. Doctor Dave declared her "cured" this Monday morning. Doctors aren't all that smart: Baby wouldn't work. We tried all types of therapy and she refused to run. She had "Drive Overflow" and then "Sector Not Found," then she had a bad command. She asked if I wanted to "Abort, Retry or Ignore." That sounds like something my gynecologist might say. I'm thinking lobotomy!

Oh, the innocent days before computers. I learned to type on an Underwood #5. We'd rewind that ribbon sixteen times. Letters looked scurrilous but nobody cared because their letters looked just as bad. Nothing ever broke on that typewriter—but now, I am spoiled!

We'd tried just about everything: Dave had walked me through several fix-it disks. He gave up and I had breakfast. I turned the infernal machine on an hour later and, lo and behold! It worked! The only problem as I can see it is that all my *Beacon* articles are now in David's "Will and Trust" file. Does this make them real official legal documents?

Update: For years we have had his and her computers. This led to separate offices...

Did John Steinbeck Have My Problems?
September 1990

Illusions of grandeur aside, I'll bet John Steinbeck never suffered for the Man as I have done in the past few weeks. I'll admit that my "Travels with David" don't compare to his *Travels With Charley* but I could add a few more chapters and verses.

Arrived in Orlando to battle the throngs of early morning office workers on their way to their cubicles and cubbyholes. The ladies wore their purple silks and matching tights and high-heeled sneakers and the men flung their ties over their shoulders and wrestled bulky briefcases and tattered folders. This was an alien world—one from which I thought I had successfully, if amicably, divorced myself a few years before. I deposited David at the appropriate air-lock and hied myself back to his parents' house to do some serious writing. "Serious" to me means getting margins lined up.

I was sitting there on a screened porch—the model of domesticity with my lap-top computer on my lap top. I'd brought an adapter so I could plug it into the wall. Unfortunately, the outlets had only two holes and my plug required three. Undaunted, I decided to use the battery option—which lasted all of one page. I could see the words fade before my eyes. Words of great wisdom, now donated to the netherworld of my memory. Son David suggested that I use a heavy-duty extension cord from the kitchen but I was afraid I'd reverse the polarity of my prima donna machine and she would wreak her havoc on the already recorded tomes. If you know Susie like they know Susie, you'd know what happened next: I had a fit. Then I collected pillows, cushions, telephone books and piled them on a lovely antique side chair and scooted it up against the kitchen cabinet where lurked one of the three pronged outlets. And I wrote. And wrote. Since I didn't have a printer, I simply saved this stuff for the time when I returned home to civilization.

Robin called yesterday: "Where is that thing you wrote?" It was pretty obvious she didn't have it from the tone of her voice. There's this thing about computers: "It's here someplace," I said. I traveled through "Garden Club," "Sierra Club," "Beacon" and "Business," "Letters Home," and a few other files. How did I file it? This morning I found it, got the printer to work—which is no mean feat—and was on the last page when David came in and suggested that I find another speaker for September 25th. So much for the article on the up-coming speaker! The rats were deserting the ship! Rewrite that article again? Forget that Noise!

Steinbeck used a portable typewriter, took no notes (and if he did, didn't use them). I know why—he couldn't find them when he wanted them. I've carefully recorded people's names—usually on matchbook covers and napkins—and inside cuffs. I've tried tape recorders—but the only satisfaction I have from that is the predictable Rolling Stones' concert when I turn it on during the Invocation.

Today, I sat down to do some more "serious writing." Dave needed an envelope done and a letter written. My thingy doesn't like envelopes and David doesn't understand. We cursored and we cursed. We chewed up envelopes and spewed venom into the stratosphere.

I said: "Honey, I love you but would you get out of this room and not try to teach me how to use my keyboard?" I was reminded a little of Ernest Hemingway.

Dave came home several days ago after being towed around

by a giant fish. Our neighbor met this same monster out back with a heftier boat than our canoe. I'd suggested that either of them take a net the next time. There was something *unmanly* about canoeing with a net, but finally they caught sight of the prey: a washtub size ray. Of which someday I may write.

There are wonders in this world of the written word. Marvels of the Muse. When I can find it on a disk I am happier than a puppy with a long lost bone. So feel for me, ache for me, laugh at me for my peccadilloes. As a good friend once asked a new acquaintance: "Have you ever tried to write?"

Mamas, Don't Let Your Babies Grow Up To Be Writers (Let Them Be Accountants or Cowboys, or Such)
October 1991

Writers
are such messy people. I knew I had earned the title when I looked around this room-of-no-return. That's all I could do—look—because to move (except to swivel in the chair) might have caused the Richter scale to document Cedar Key's first earthquake. It's not that writers are disorganized or even unorganized. It's just that we are born sloppy. I'll kill for the right adjective–it's probably right here under a cat someplace!

Edna Ferber (or was it Pearl Buck?) explained that the only difference between a writer and a non-writer is that a writer writes. Profound statement—whichever lady said it. What she didn't say is that writing is such a messy procedure.

It used to be that I could write a reasonable sentence without ripping apart a house. David taught me to research. This means that I save every scrap of paper that comes through the mail, newspapers and cents-off coupons. People even bring me their old editions of the *Beacon*. We don't recycle paper in my house, we digest it.

Words bother me. The English language is so beautiful because we have so many ways to say the same thing. Innuendo is the thing to worry about. I was poised in the "write" mode but couldn't think of the word I wanted. David appeared at the door.

"Give me an A-word that means that I want to tell somebody that they aren't right in what they are thinking. I want to Dis-them of their idea."

"Susan, do you want lunch or what? Try Disavow."

"No!" (I'd already disabused myself of "disavow.")

"Try Disabuse"

"Why didn't I think of that?"

"Now, do you want lunch or shall I disabuse you of the notion?"

Contrary to the popular opinion, writing is not lonely. The cast of characters that waltzes across my adrenal cortex rivals that of a C. B. DeMille epic. Fiction and Fact, from Susan's Almanac! Lonely, no. Reclusive, yes. I find myself enjoying swiveling about in my chair unable to reach farther than the telephone. I put cryptic notes on my doors that everyone ignores—they know I am in here doing nothing more than puttering. Puttering is what I call it when faced with shoveling out the room. Each box of pictures is worth many thousands of words, matched only by the many thousands of words stacked in the other corner. Stapler, scotch tape and push pins go in the jar, not in the carpet. Do I really need an industrial-strength paper cutter as a door stop? Really, just really, who tried to sharpen a cigarette in my pencil sharpener? Did I do that in a fit of pique? Scraps of paper with names and phone numbers could probably put me in jail.

Writing is so much fun. The laundry is whirring away, the dishwasher gobbling the goblets. The LSO (Legalized Significant Other) is due to arrive—and ignore my note on the door—in approximately eight hours. Between now and then, I will have to think of something to write. Deadlines are Deadlines!

Cedar Key Living

Water Under the Number 4 Bridge

How Do You Find Cedar Key?

Did you ever try telling anyone how to get to Cedar Key?

Normally intelligent people start blithering when you snake them through Levy County, away from anything that looks like an interstate highway system. They simply refuse to believe that flowers still grow on roadsides and that turtles still cross roads on foot.

My friend, Joan, is a good example. I sent her a map. I'll admit I am neither a Rand or McNally and am a particularly bad artist, but considering the number of times Dave and I have traversed those 150 miles to and from Orlando, I should think it would inspire confidence. She called and told me that she'd wind up in Harrisburg, Pennsylvania, following my directions.

I'd counted miles from US 27 and memorized the names of the horse farms. I knew which Circle K's were offering "Big Gulps" of liquid. Joan then asked, "Are there any bridges in Cedar Key?" I admitted that there were a few. "I don't cross bridges," she said.

Son David has visited many times. Each time he comes a different way. He shows up at the back door for unexplained reasons. He's fine with directions as long as it is a turnpike or the road reads "Interstate Something." He at least points his truck west and winds up in Cedar Key. It has to be the homing instinct.

Cedar Key is really not hard to find. A few months ago I ordered lily bulbs from Holland. The Dutch do not worry about bridges. The man from UPS must have simply stood on the Number Four Bridge and shouted, "Who ordered these lilies?" Steven, with his wry humor, told me that Eve didn't have a street address on her apple tree either.

I don't think that I am an inhospitable hostess. I'll suggest that my guests bring double-wide sleeping bags and a gallon of Avon Skin-so-Soft. I turn off the sprinkler when I see someone drive in the driveway and leash the attack cats. I put the shotgun behind the door. I try so hard! Welcome to my world!

Plenty To Do in Cedar Key
March 1989

When I first moved to Cedar Key as a permanent, full-time, year-round resident, I got some mighty strange responses from my city friends. "What will you do?" I usually gave them a smirky little grin and said, "As little as possible."

Others would try to be a little more savant: "Oh, you must like to fish a lot."

"Well, yes, but I'm not really very good at it." I didn't try to explain the motives behind tearing myself away from Mall World, and their ribbons of frustration they call city streets.

My intention to do as little as possible has turned into something of a joke. There are not enough hours of the day to do everything I'd like to do in this community.

I concluded a long time ago that bored people must be boring people and I cannot remember the last time I was bored.

Activities here are a little different from those in the big cities. We are more people oriented. Instead of waiting for the postal delivery, we go to the post office, meet our neighbors, chat over a bin of tomatoes at James' vegetable stand. We might argue the virtue of a new ordinance on the street corner; we'll pop into the market for an item or two, and see a couple more neighbors.

While this is quite a bit more fun than standing in a high-tech check-out line with a uniformed cashier, it is not exactly what city friends would consider "activity."

Except for the usual weekend visitors there are community activities that are totally absorbing. So much so, that it is easy to get in over one's head.

When we first moved here, our youngest son was still in high school. It didn't take me long to find out that this one, like every other school, needs volunteer help. There are some pretty exciting games and meets to attend. Just because the school is small doesn't mean it takes a back seat to anyone. You'll get the Shark Spirit in a hurry. I think it's something they put in the popcorn!

Once upon a time Dave and I joined the Orange County Historical Society. We were interested but the meetings were held ten miles away, had a Board the size of the University of Florida faculty. Even though at the time Dave was a forty-year resident of Orlando, we never got around to attending a meeting; visited the museum occasionally.

We would read the newsletter and say, "We really should go."

Cedar Key has an active and exciting historical society and museum. You will see the board members at the post office any day of the week. The museum is small and jam-packed with Cedar Key history. Many of the society's members are either visitors or winter residents of Cedar Key. This does not mean that they do not contribute time, energy and talent while here.

I'm fond of our little library—temporarily displaced due to the renovation of City Hall. Diane knows her books and in time will know you as a patron and direct you to what you like. The Friends of the Library try to keep current books on the shelves, up-to-date magazines. They have wonderful sales at least once a year where you may buy back the books you've inadvertently donated.

Cedar Key has an active Women's Club and a Garden Club who do their part to keep Cedar Key the way Cedar Key was meant to be. The Lions and Lionesses put on the big shows of the year: the Seafood Festival in October and assist with the Art Festival Committee in April. They work year-round to organize these festivals, coordinating churches, school and other groups for the successful venture.

The new kid on the block is the Eagles Aerie 4194. This is more than a social club and assists needy families through its fund raising projects.

Growing up in large cathedral-style church, I was a member of the church choir for probably ten years before I realized I couldn't sing. Not exactly tone-deaf, I came across like Willie Nelson doing Ave Maria. One of my children inherited my ability; the other two, their father's clear baritone. In Cedar Key, we all sing! We carol at Christmas, have Cantatas at Easter, regardless of Church affiliation.

Let no one say there is "nothing to do" in Cedar Key. Plant a radish, take in a stray cat. Visit a city council meeting. You won't ever be bored! Marvel at the sky, tingle at the temperatures. There's more to Cedar Key than fish!

Another Side of the Mailbox
November 1989

Dear Editor:

Perhaps I will incur the wrath of my "salty" publisher but variety of opinion is the spice of Cedar Key.

For myself, I enjoy telling people that I live in a large post office box and that the postmaster feeds me once a day. I have no desire to have home delivery of my mail. For me, the eternally vigilant frugal person, home delivery of mail is a frill I can do without. If I could mail a letter with my still-crisp three-cent stamps I would do so. Why should I buy a mailbox, pay a letter carrier's gasoline to bring me my mail, when I am still capable of going to a central location?

Maybe it is my perverse sense of humor, but I enjoy telling officials that I have no street address. Postmaster Joe and I made up one for telephone purposes. It doesn't jive with anything else they have on record but it made their computer happy at least for the moment.

I don't have any problem with people finding me in Cedar Key. They just go downtown and shout—or if they are of a brighter nature, they call me on the telephone before venturing to my residence. Phone calls cost exactly the same as stamps!

If parking is a problem in front of the post office, it is partly because someone designated two handicapped spaces for the occasional user. It takes only minutes to retrieve mail from a box and perhaps the handicapped person would be one who would benefit from home delivery.

There are lots of funny little traditions in this very special town. Let's not mess with the ones like visiting with neighbors at the post office!

Susan Roquemore, Cedar Key

If This Is Fantasyland,
I'm Sure Not Sleeping Beauty
November 1990

Sometimes, when I am hoisting bags of groceries up the stairs, I do compare my house to Cinderella's castle for sheer height. My hair isn't quite long enough to toss over the deck like Rapunzel did and there aren't many dwarfs singing "Hi Ho" (the closest I get is an owl saying "Whoo-Whoo").

Still, I recall sitting around with a new acquaintance one day talking about the ways of Levy County—such high-minded conversations I find myself engaged in—when he could contain himself no longer: "Who are you to say that? You're from Cedar Key—and that place is Fantasyland!"

Well, it takes a lot to put the brakes on my tongue but that statement put the whole body in irons.

As this new friend was a professional educator, our conversation was mainly about schools. Admittedly, I was bragging about our dandy little school. I was bragging about the people who saved it, time after time, from closure and how with minimum funds provided, it provided personalized education for the students. I knew from personal experience that it allowed students—even pushed those not otherwise inclined—into participating in sports and running for class offices. It allowed them to walk to school, eat lunch under the trees. Teachers and parents were on a first name basis. It was always "Miss Susan" or "Miss Kathy" or "Miss Jane." That we had our fair share of dropouts was to be offset by our fair share of National Merit Scholars.

"Fantasyland?" I regained use of my tongue. "Why?" I wondered aloud.

"You people just do things differently, that's all." And, you know, he was right and is right.

There's not a whole lot of money to go around in Cedar Key or Levy County or even in the whole country right now. So perhaps it is easier to make do with little in this fantasy-world—operate on a shoestring—than in other places.

I've been searching for the right word to describe people who live in Cedar Key: tenacious, bull-headed, tough, arrogant. Cedar

Key rarely chooses its people: the people choose Cedar Key. She is a harsh mistress at times. So what is the siren song of Cedar Key? Why do people choose to come to this ancient sand dune? It's not for the climate, which can be muggy, sticky, stormy and sometimes downright cold. It's not for the manicured landscaping of hills and valleys and lawns. It could be for the lure of the sea, but there are other places with better access to the water and beaches. It certainly isn't a planned community. Still, I chose the fantasy and am living it.

Our Own Little Blood Factory!!
June 1989

Maybe it was because it was raining and I didn't have anything better to do. Maybe it was because I didn't want to go home and do dishes, wasn't in a mood to cook (and didn't have a clean pot anyway). Maybe it was one of those rare bursts of altruism that came upon me without warning. Whatever the motivation, I stopped in at the Bloodmobile parked next to City Hall last week.

Giving blood is no new thing to me. As a college student I supported my toothpaste habit by donating to the new Open Heart Unit at what was then J. Hillis Miller Health Center. I was as regular as the transients who stand in front of any plasma center. No one seemed to notice those tell-tale band-aids at regular intervals. No one except David—who thought the practice pretty ghoulish. (We almost didn't get married due to the required blood test.) Time passed, and I got out of the habit of dropping in occasionally at the blood bank. I was either pregnant or had the flu (or both), underweight or just had a vaccination. There was always a good reason not to go.

The first thing that happened this day was that I was met by two young ladies who gave me a ream of questions to answer. I would have done better with cards done in Braille. I'd left the reading glasses in the car. One of them read the questions to me. I hadn't had anybody read to me since I was four years old. I felt a little foolish and a little old. We were doing fine with the questions about being pregnant or having VD, but were stalled on traveling habits. No one seemed to be able to find Egypt and without my glasses, the closest I could come was to point out the Nile River. "That is in Asia?" When I told her it was North Africa she envisioned tsetse flies and dengue fever. I decided discretion was the better part of valor and let her entertain her own thoughts. I wasn't about to tell her what I ate in the Middle East.

I assured her that the mosquitoes in Cedar Key are far more potent than those I encountered in the "jungles" of Africa.

Our next order of business was for me to show her my one and only good vein. She was suspect and inspected the left antecubital plexus as well.

"Just like a spider web," she murmured.

"Uh hum."

She slipped a cuff around the good arm and whiz bang—she found some blood! This girl might not be able to find Egypt, but she sure was good at drawing blood. I told her that it would be a very slow draw. I was hoping she wasn't impatient and I wouldn't still be sitting there at closing time. I wasn't. She unhooked me, gave me some California-tasting orange juice and I went home to take the nap she suggested. This girl really was good.

As I was departing, she said, "What do people in Cedar Key do around here anyway?" I said, "When we get really bored, we give blood!"

What a Good Idea!

The first time I saw a telethon I thought, "What a good idea." Television auctions for the benefit of this or that worthy cause made my heart go pitter-pat. I bought a block of tickets for an Orlando Blazers game. For those of you who can remember the Orlando Blazers (I think it was a football team), you might also remember when we called Orange Avenue that because there were orange trees on it. Heck, I'm old enough to remember the Tampa Smokers. (No joke and that was a baseball team!) Tampa was making cigars in those days with Cuban leaf tobacco. I'm beginning to believe that I pre-date the cold war and have outlived it. I did and have and so there!

I like good ideas but tend to say: "Let's see if it works." Frankly, I didn't think the postal system would work either back when Ben and I discussed it.

We are going to be (and already are) faced with the problem of doing things for our own communities in the most painless way we can separate ourselves from our checkbooks. I'm such an anarchist that I don't even believe that we should rely on government to pave roads or subsidize my kid's education. But as long as those avenues are already there, well, why not..? Thank goodness none of my children have political aspirations. Their mom would be a definite "Miss Susannah says..."

It was then with some degree of snarlerism that I wondered why in the world anyone would want to do anything with that wonderful auditorium at Cedar Key School. (Only a few short years ago it was called Cedar Key High School, even though it housed many more grades!) It was exactly as I remembered my first grade auditorium in 1948 (the Cedar Key School building dates to 1951). Broward School in Tampa probably was older than our principal was and she was probably at least 40 at the time. The fact that I didn't have a very happy first grade experience probably warped me for all time, but when I sat down in the Cedar Key School seats, I was back there with my blue construction-paper-covered report card with a butterfly sticker getting torn by a seat in front of me. I was there waiting for my brother who was supposed to ride me home on his bike. I was there with the leftover and very hot woolen bunny ears waiting for my line in the first grade play. I was there to watch my son receive his high school diploma. We did very nicely, thank you.

Nobody expected air conditioning in 1948. Sweat was good for the soul (my parents told me).

Even in the '60s, few buildings were cooled at the University of Florida. Perhaps that's why we had so many medically-oriented and business-oriented graduates that season! Maybe that's why so many of us headed for Cedar Key! I hate to think of anything less than 50 years old as being antiquated and I sure don't want to spoil the flavor of that grand auditorium with all its tasty memories.

Let's go ahead and do something for this school, these young-uns, these today people. Let's put them in comfortable seats so that they can hear their principal award their awards. Let's not begrudge them a quiet air conditioning unit Let's give them a stage to perform on and a curtain that doesn't drop except on cue. Let's bring Cedar Key School our of my Twilight Zone. Steve doesn't know it yet, but he just bought a seat in the new auditorium. The Class of '88 had four seniors. Boys. Men. Jerald, Lamar, Jimmy, Steve. Those fellows could rebuild the world given enough food. Let's find those others who had their first grade report card torn or who broke out in a rash with the wooly bunny ears. Cedar Key School is special.

Years after I wrote this article, a major part of Cedar Key School was destroyed by fire (again). Investigation indicated that the fire started in the auditorium ceiling, perhaps from faulty wiring.

There's a World Between a Visitor And a Tourist

Did you ever notice that I refer to people who come to Cedar Key as "Visitors," not "Tourists"? The word "Tourist" conjures up images of my old home in "Tourist-World": Father yanking Junior's shoulder out of the socket dragging him along and baby screaming on mother's hip. They enter any eating establishment dripping sweat and ice-cream and begin by complaining about the weather (it can be a balmy January and they are missing the snow or a rainy day in July and they are missing a drought back home) but you can be sure the Tourist will find the weather objectionable in Florida. And, apparently their mosquitoes at home don't bite, either.

Visitor, on the other hand, might smile secretly (and superiorly) that we do indeed wear white shoes before Easter, but they don't seem to mind. Their kids get mopped up before entering an art gallery. They leave the remnant of the cone outside as well.

Tourist should not be such an ugly word—after all, it is merely descriptive of one who tours. To me, it connotes a person, family or group racing from one place to the other, never stopping long enough to crunch a camphor tree leaf to smell or put a daisy in a Seven-Up bottle.

Tourists are always in a hurry. They eat fast, talk loud, push little kids out of the way so see the parade and leave early. Tourists are boors. They are probably boors at home as well.

A Visitor visits. He, she, they have invited themselves into your home. They are to be treated as guests. They will be fed, watered, pampered with the utmost hospitality. Visitors are not purchased for the price of an admission ticket or a room fee or a restaurant tab or tip. A Visitor is honored and welcomed and welcomed back.

For the most part, at least on calm, normal weeks, the people that come to Cedar Key are Visitors. They sweat just as much as the Tourists do and just as much as the residents. Their feet get sore from walking and maybe they sunburn a little more than do we who live here. Mosquitoes bite them. They don't catch as many fish as they have read about. They try mullet for breakfast *with grits*. They don't throw cans into the water. Visitors are treasures worth more than pirate gold.

It's been my experience—and I used to call myself a Tourist before I knew the difference—that traveling is a pretty exciting thing to do as long as you roll with the flow. Get into the spirit, but don't tell folks, "That's not the way we do it back home." If siesta time is at noon, try a siesta! If the locals eat at 10 PM, have peanut butter and jelly at six and wait for the main course at ten and expect to be served at midnight. It's really a lot of fun to make the transition from being a Tourist to being a Visitor and then to the title "Traveler."

Cedar Key welcomes its Visitors. We welcome our Tourists if they try to understand that this is not a theme park created for amusement. We have no roller coasters or trained porpoises. What you see is what you get, and it's usually a lot for the money if you look in the right places.

This Was the Week That Was (and Is!)
April 1990

Festival

Week in Cedar Key is akin to every bazaar you ever attended; every bake sale; every basketball game; every four-year-old's birthday party. It's like July 4th and Christmas. It's a garage sale without the garage. It's corn dogs and chocolate chip cookies, lemonade and peanuts. It's a fish fry. It's watching teenagers whomp up a batch of clam fritters. It's seeing the athletes dole out smoked mullet to the uninitiated. It's joking with the PTO men and women about when they are going to run out of shrimp. It's blowing the hamburger-charcoal smoke out of your face as you stand behind their grill trying to make change. Senior Betas will make fish cakes. I'll have to stop eating this very day to start sampling this food. This year, the office of the school has gotten into the act. Sooner or later, everyone does! They are doing ice cream!

Lest we forget, this is an Art Festival! Cedar Key's Main Street will be lined with fine art: over two hundred exhibitors will have booths ranging from oils to collage. Items range from the pricey to the downright affordable. It all depends on what you like. These, generally, are artists who like to talk about their work. They enjoy festivals. They enjoy Cedar Key. Stop and chat with them. Find out what makes them tick, if you can. Buy a bag of peanuts (biodegradable) and a book. Curl into your hostel bed after a festival day knowing that you have experienced a piece of Americana—a love suite that few other communities can ever provide. Don't be bitter or angry. Don't wish what was not meant to be. Be happy that you for a brief time have known Cedar Key.

It is the people of Cedar Key that make the festival—each festival, rain or shine—an event to remember. Not just club members but their spouses are drafted into duty. Proprietors of shops and restaurants don't run and hide when they see that "I need" look in a customer's eye.

The Friends of the Library needed a platform on which to put what looked like a million pounds of books. Cook's Cafe lent saw-horses and heavy plywood. Harry Hooper found just the right donation jar in his back room when asked. He even threw in a couple of pickle jars if the library needed them.

The Garden Club was for a moment concerned that the sign-up list was missing. Chairman Annette Haven was non-plussed. "People will remember," she said. The Garden Club President rolled her eyes skyward and prayed a silent prayer to the god of festivals that she was right.

People don't always know what it means to put on a festival in a town the size of Cedar Key. There are approximately eight-hundred residents, but these are hard to count since some of the most vital citizens might not be here the full year. They'll work all winter for an organization only to leave just before or just after the Spring Festival. The organizers have to keep a calendar of who will be here when. Too, many of the Cedar Keyans are of an independent spirit and leave the island to visit friends or relatives at a moment's notice. Some of us just take off for no good reason whatsoever. Somehow, the Festival works. It works wonders, it re-vitalizes us.

Down on Main Street, crews were sprucing up the lawn in front of City Hall. These were not city crews, for we boast only a handful of workers who do everything from change light bulbs to paving our streets. These young women were from Lancaster Correctional Institution and need to be thanked for the care they gave our town, and hope they return under more auspicious circumstances.

We've instructed our birds to be on their best behavior. They should not squawk before dawn. Our pelicans will be picturesque but won't bite anyone's nose off. We've discussed weather with Mother Nature and she says that her computer is down. This seems to be a fairly normal week in Cedar Key.

For me, I reckon I should lay in a supply of sleeping bags. My friends tend to enjoy *roughing it* here in the provinces.

Tuning In to Festival Sights and Sounds
October 1988

Blame

it on the fact that I am an inveterate eavesdropper. I learned to tune into conversations in restaurants, restrooms and at rest areas when I was a toddler. It provided humor, education and sometimes a sense of pathos. Although I have not elevated it to an art form, I'm pretty good at it.

How many people took pictures at the Seafood Festival? Lots! How many people listened to the sounds of the festival? Oh, I don't mean the boom, boom of the cannons or the Gospel music; I mean the conversations! Without benefit of a tape-recorder, I will give you a sampling of the profound things I heard and loved.

Two young men accompanied by their ladies: "I *hate* going places like this with girls. You all want to *look* at everything!"

"Does this fish have bones?"

"Is there a fish market in Cedar Key?"

"I want to buy back the book I donated last year."

"If you buy it, where will you put it?" (About a paper parrot).

"If you are leaving, can I have your parking space?"

"What's happening today?" (This from a non-suspecting Ocala couple.)

"Can you drink beer here?" Answer: You'll find out!

It was a good-humored crowd of people that came to town for the festival last weekend. Cedar Key is not a place that people have to come to, they *want* to come!

It is also a time for local people to see each other sweating behind booths together, elbow-deep in mystic batters. People making change without the benefit of cash registers and the sounds of orders being placed.

"We sold out of *everything*!" sighed a PTO member.

"I've got the raffle tickets right here on my body," said a high school Booster member.

"Should I knock first?" asked a lady standing in front of a porta-potty.

There were a few unpleasant sounds, but very few. As a young lady was being placed in an ambulance, the attendant said with justifiable terseness: "You know as much as I do" to the query, "What happened to her?"

There was an unpleasant honking of a horn on Highway 24

entering Cedar Key on Sunday afternoon about 3 PM. Now why would anyone in bumper-to-bumper traffic honk a horn? Did they expect to speed up Cedar Key?

The sound of cars rushing by, starting the night before the festival, did not interrupt my sleep but was unpleasant inasmuch as I have accustomed myself to being awakened by sunshine or moonglow. It was reminiscent of the sounds of my mother's house near Interstate 75.

As we were leaving the festival Sunday I thought it might be fun to see how many planes were on the airstrip. The young man asked us: "You sightseeing, taking a ride or what?" I did think that his query could have been couched in friendlier terms. No matter, but I do listen to words, and how they are said.

A friend popped a pop-gun next to us as we were browsing. I jumped a foot! And threatened to "shoot her" with the camera. This is festival spirit, and is the essence of the joy that emanates from these occasions.

It was the sound of Ruth Wagner in the Historical Society Museum patiently explaining some finer points of history to a patron and the sound of a baby in a stroller gurgling and burping and doing the things that babies do.

It was a lively quiet. It was a quiet lively.

Festivals are sights and lights. Festivals are parades, contests and sales. Festivals are pageants. Festivals are food. Festivals are sounds. It is the neighborly voice of a friend asking: "Can you help me take the tarp down?"

"Till next Spring?"

White Powder

Junior Smith was one of our City Commissioners. He was a burly man, gruff of speech, bluff of temperament, white-haired and red-faced. Women got the idea that he expected them to stay home and be quiet. That was never my style although I have to admit staying home appealed to me more than being quiet. Junior had a way of rattling cages of people who wrote for the newspaper.

It was in this frame of mind that Robin Raftis and I engaged in one of the first and only practical jokes I'd ever perpetrated. It started innocently enough. I was at the time either President or Vice President of the Garden Club. We'd had a little bit of a problem with the sugar supply at the last festival and had to use powdered sugar for a few hours until we could replenish with granulated. (You just don't understand how hard it was to get supplies to this town back then!) The point is, I had forty pounds of powdered sugar to get rid of after the festival. I bagged it all up in zip-lock bags, weighed it out in my kitchen and took two or three pint bags to the *Beacon* office. I left them on Robin's desk, saying "What should I do with this? I've got forty pounds of it!"

Robin Raftis, then the managing editor of the *Beacon*, had a wicked sense of humor and an utter talent for riling the Commission, especially Junior. She grabbed one of my baggies and met Junior in the street during the lunch hour. In broad daylight she says to him: "Look what Sue Roquemore brought in." (It was a pound by my kitchen scale—a little less than half a kilo—nice white powder.) That ruddy man turned as white as his hair. He visibly recoiled and refused to touch it. "Get that stuff away from me."

It really *was* mean of us to do that. The Feds had just done a major bust of a drug operation outside Cedar Key. The town was reeling from that sting. And here we were, playing games. Naughty but oh, so much fun.

Lost in Downtown Cedar Key!?!
August 1989

A few years ago a fellow named Donald Westlake wrote a book about a band of inept crooks who could do nothing right. In one episode, they, instead of robbing a bank, decided to steal the bank itself, building and all, and lost it. Never mind that the bank was housed in a temporary building at the time or that it inadvertently rolled into the water and was lost to all concerned, including the robbers. (It was a pretty funny book.)

It's getting almost like that going into downtown Cedar Key

these days! For the last few months, City Hall was in the old library space. The library was in the Strong House behind the museum. The museum offices were in the process of being moved to an addition.

I thought I had all of this neatly sorted out in my somewhat webby brain. I wasn't sure when I left that stack of books at what had been City Hall (the library now) whether Frances Hodges would be reading *Art Critic* magazines for months to come. Indeed, would she think I was hinting at buying sculptures for the front lawn?

One day I innocently walked into the museum office and saw only space where the files had been kept. Eek! Who made off with the side of the building?

Today came the latest surprise: I was delivering late copy to the *Beacon* office. I am used to dashing in at odd hours, stuffing the material into the box and making a hasty retreat before I can be caught by an editor wielding a blue pencil. Robin was faster than I was. In the course of our conversation she said, "We're moving." I'm certain they are trying to stay one step ahead of me.

Even our bank tried to outfox me one time. Their return address was something like South West 163rd Street, Cedar Key. Dave and I pictured this someplace between Seahorse Key and the Yucatan Peninsula. We agreed that this was carrying branch banking to its extreme. His sly grin told me that it just might cut down on the checks written for "Cash."

Why do I have this nagging suspicion that someone is trying to tell me something? When my confessor leaves without a forwarding address, I will know that I am in deep trouble!

I Want To Vote in Cedar Key
May 1990

Dear Editor:

By nature I'm not a very political animal. The last time I ran for anything, it was painted yellow and had four wheels and I didn't catch it. Like other people I'd rather stand by and gripe about the state of the state than put my psyche on the line to try and change anything.

That's only partially true since I value my right to vote almost as much as I value my right as a woman to have a tantrum now and then. There were some difficult choices to make in this last election—the few choices that I was allowed to make at least were difficult. You see, even though I think of myself as a Cedar Key resident and throw myself wholeheartedly into things in Cedar Key, I am still a second-class citizen. I cannot vote in city elections. It is really ironic that Dave and I have only lived in one house in all our years together within city limits. For twenty-two years we resided within a stone's throw of the Orlando line. The situation was entirely different since we were in the hub of Orange County's protection. Here we depend upon Cedar Key's services: police, fire, water, sewage and all the rest. I travel the streets daily and while I'll admit I do little to tear up the pavement, I do my limited share of wear and tear.

More than that I truly care about the future of this marvelous city. I have strong feelings about growth management. Dave and I feel the aches and pains of the community. We know the tax base is fragile. Leadership in Cedar Key is probably more tricky than any other place in Florida. To those people entrusted with guiding Cedar Key for the next few years, I offer a hope and a prayer. By the time this is printed, we will know who you are.

Some of us would like to have a voice next time around.

My neighbors may not appreciate my sentiments. It might cost them a few more dollars a year. I for one would like to use Cedar Key as my return address and know that I am truly part of the community, voting privileges and all the rest. I can think of worse ways to spend a buck.

Susan Roquemore, Boogie Ridge

Walter Beckham's small island, next to Highway 24 and contiguous to the city, was annexed as part of Cedar Key in December 1992, and we petitioned (successfully) for annexation shortly after. In the voting for City Council which had concluded just before our annexation, "Salty" Raftis was defeated by one vote.

Old Dogs, New Tricks, There's No Place Like Home
August 1991

It seems appropriate at this time each year to take stock of my mental status since it was on a clear hot steamy August day that the Roquemores moved to Cedar Key. "Have you taken leave of your senses?" was the common refrain (and this was from the people in Cedar Key). Most of the Orlando folks just shook their heads in tandem and sighed, "There they go again."

Maybe it was just that it was the only way to get the house cleaned out once and for all, and maybe it was because we sought new adventures without dodging terrorists in foreign airports, but Cedar Key sounded like the 99% Solution.

We really weren't strangers to the island and contrary to popular opinion were not just driving through on our way to Mexico. Living in Cedar Key "full time" is trip enough for any lifetime.

There were quite a few things to be learned from living in this town and most of these were absorbed by osmosis. One of the first things I learned is that every place is long-distance. Southern Bell's stock rose to bullish proportions as did the length and breadth of our phone bill. The long distance of the road was rather a treat than a treatment. I found that I could get to Gainesville in the time it took me to get to a shopping mall in Orlando and that the drive was decidedly more pleasant (if you stay out of the way of errant deer). Never before had I had a post office box. It was one of those few things that David and I argued about. To live without home delivery? That is downright uncivilized! We learned about Cedar Key weather. Even the garden catalogs can't decide whether we are North or South or Central or Gulf Coastal or a combination of Northwest-Central-Coastal. No wonder. God can't figure it out, either. Cedar Key enjoys a reputation for storms. It's a humdinger of a reputation that pits flood insurance against wind-storm insurance against a very skinny purse. No such problem existed in honest-to-goodness Central Florida. Trees regularly fell over—once on my neighbor's car which was parked in our communal drive. It was decided that it was our tree. No one knew for sure but the insurance companies vied for the privilege of soaking one of us.

Cedar Key weather can be hot or cold but rarely at the same

time. Never did I expect to be scraping snow off my decks only weeks after sustaining a sunburn.

Shortly after moving here Dave announced: "There are no birds in Cedar Key!" (He doesn't consider pelicans "birds," but that is another story.) "David, darling, this is a bird sanctuary—they are all in the trees praying!" There are all kinds of birds in Cedar Key, but our problem was that we didn't recognize half of them. The usual confluence of bluejays and mockingbirds hadn't found us. Neither had the cardinals, the thrashers and the towhees. Instead weird little twitterers and giant ospreys, owls, eagles, anhingas, ibis soared around. Never in my life had I seen so many robins as in that first garden.

Having raised three sons to manhood and paid my dues in quite a few schools, the Cedar Key school was a refreshing change. Unless you've attended a game at a large school you won't understand the unabashed joy of being able to cheer for a name rather than a number. We tried to get the graduating class declared smallest in the United States but some private school someplace beat us for the honor. Honor it was. Distinction, certainly.

Some of the things I took for granted in a large town are impossible here. Just try to get a Mazda fixed. Don't expect to buy stamps after noon on Thursdays. Only two people in the town smoke Virginia Slims 120 Menthols, so if the stores are out, they are *out* (maybe they are telling me to quit, anyway). I learned the pleasure of nodding to neighbors and strangers alike.

Cedar Key is a very small town with some big-city problems. I learned this in a hurry. Where I live, we don't even have cable TV. Now, that is a major deficiency! The things we learned were worth doing without the Simpsons.

Mullet eating is worthy of note. I'd grown up with grits for breakfast, but mullet? The fish? It wasn't long before I realized that mullet makes a great breakfast and until you've eaten Cedar Key mullet you ain't arrived. In a crust so light, with the fish so juicy and flaky that it melts on the fork, I scream that for the first forty-four years of my life I didn't meet a mullet on a plate before noon.

There are probably some other things I learned along the byways of the last four years. One of these is, if you don't tell, I won't. There's no place like home, and no home like Cedar Key.

Never ever say "never." The day came when David and I gave our hearts (and a good portion of our checkbook) to a cabin in the foothills of the Virginia Blue Ridge. For the next ten years, we added rooms; we built sweat equity in what we now call "Justa Cabin." For ten years plus, every time we made a non-critical building boo-boo we'd say: "Well, after all, it is just a cabin..."

The Pelican Brief
My red face lives on in memory

Reviled by some for his unkempt appearance and perceived attempts at "panhandling" but loved and appreciated by others for his love for things wild, Owen Freeman was a Cedar Key fixture for years. The "best friend" of our pelicans, he spent the last years of his life saving them, when he could, from the dangers of modern life.

When I was still relatively new to Cedar Key and maybe before I even started writing for the *Beacon* I'd hang out down on the big dock and watch the birds and the fishermen. I'd take pictures. Steven and I would walk around collecting weeds for my flower arrangements (Mom's Weeds of the Week). I watched this man hurl cast after cast out from the dock and bring in more than one big bird. *I was appalled. I was incensed. I was infuriated.* I wrote a scathing letter to the newspaper talking about this insensitive clod. This man was Owen—who was retrieving birds whose necks were wrapped with monofilament line. He'd bring them in, help them, untangle them and treat them if they were starved. Of course I didn't know that at the time. I was told and I was apologetic. To this day Owen remembers my public apology. I, however, have never forgotten what it is like to make a total ass of myself in print. He was gracious—he said that he knew I cared about the birds—which is what he was doing too.

You might see Owen around town on his scooter these days. Back then he used a bicycle. Don't you dare sneer—he knows more about birds than you and I will ever begin to know and he will care a whole lot more. He just doesn't look too pretty doing it.

Letter to the Editor
February 1989

Dear Editor,

Last Friday I put my foot in my mouth all the way down to my gullet. I want to apologize not for what I said or how I said it, but for my own ignorance. You see, if there is one person here in Cedar Key who feels as strongly about our wildlife as Harriet Smith, it is I.

When I saw a grown man obviously "tormenting" a pelican with a small bait fish on the end of a line out on city pier, I saw shades of red and purple, electric blue and green. I asked him in no uncertain terms (and in a loud voice) how dare he "murder" that bird!

My husband and I had noticed the bird earlier—with multiple hooks in it and had tried unsuccessfully to reach Harriet. Not only had this gentleman spoken to Harriet about the bird, he knew, as I did not, what to do and how to do it!

After I left the pier, embarrassed and still frustrated by the plight of the afflicted bird, the man explained to Dave that this was the fourth bird he had so rescued that day and that there were six the day before.

My harsh words are still ringing in my ears. I would say them again but next time, I'll ask a few kind questions first.

Susan Roquemore, Cedar Key

Animal Control
August 1989

Cats, rats, dogs and coons, and even some squirrely humans can get rabies. Personally, I've never met a case of rabies outside a textbook, but that doesn't mean it isn't there lurking in a tree someplace. I've met and nursed quite a few people with leukemia and no doctor ever suggested that they caught it from a cat.

Indeed, research has shown that feline leukemia is transmissible only to other felines. Catty as I sometimes am, I refrain from eating Kozy Kitten and sitting on fences under the full moon. The worst thing I've ever caught from my cat is a hefty sneeze. In the days before feline leukemia vaccine, a very wonderful cat, Count Dracula by name, died of the virus. Veterinary medicine has progressed to protect my pets from everything except the automobile and humans.

Dogs and cats and coons and turtles and opossums and snakes and lizards and worms don't bother me a whole lot. I don't feed stray or wild anything. That includes you, buster!

Cedar Key does have a problem with roaming animals. Dogs will chase anything that runs or revolves on wheels. If this four-legged chaser weighs a hundred pounds or more and flashes a set of ivories tuned into my ankle or throat, I have cause for alarm. I will have to admit that the last time I was bitten by a dog was in my own living room and I was trying to teach a recalcitrant dachshund the manly arts of siring. His proposed bride didn't cotton to my well-meaning interference. No one with an ounce of sense would pick up an unwilling cat—I have scars to prove that sometimes my sense is measured in milligrams. Cedar Key needs some sort of animal control ordinance. For me, who believes in a government with the fewest possible rules, to say this means that even I recognize that all people are not responsible pet owners. Some people do allow their cats to reproduce geometrically. They are either stupid or uncaring not to have their animals neutered, vaccinated against rabies, leptosporosis, leukemia, heartworms, and the other creepies that cause so much misery. Pet ownership is expensive. In Cedar Key it is more than money expense—it means travel time as well. Chiefland, Gainesville and Archer have veterinarians. We do not. Besides that, who is going to haul that ole yeller dog who forages in the trash can out front to the vet? Who is going to take the nest of kittens found in the garage to the shelter?

We live in what may be the last of the wildlife refuges. Maybe we should just allow our raccoons to live like raccoons live. Maybe we should ignore the bird droppings on our car roofs and slow down for turtles crossing State Road 24. Maybe we should mourn when Ole Yeller is found in a ditch. Maybe what all of us need is a couple of tablespoons full of an organized city—complete with an animal clinic on every corner and leash laws and dogcatchers on the city payroll. It is not my idea of Utopia. Still, I don't jog and battle the dog. The pesky and healthy raccoon who lives on the island behind my house and I have a truce. He leaves my cats alone and I don't give him rabies.

Those Dear Deer on Highway 24
August 1989

They're frisky. They're lively. They are so neat to watch as they nibble on the landscape. Some people find it great sport to hunt deer for dinner table fare. While I have yet to turn down a venison steak, I'm not the great white hunter!

What happens when the deer turn the tables on us people types? We are neatly sheathed in several thousand pounds of steel and fiberglass. We are galloping by at 55 miles per hour! The result is sure not pretty.

David drives a Jeep Cherokee. It looks something like a Sherman Tank. After his encounter with the deer, it looked like a Sherman Tank that met a Panzer! The heavy duty bumper grill filled with doe-feathers!

Jimmy and Steve toddled into the driveway last Sunday afternoon with a similar story. This time the car was a sporty Mazda RX-7. If I hadn't seen the car I would have imagined the front end accordion-pleated. This particular deer decided, however, to crash head-long into the passenger door. Steve was pretty sporty himself with splattered glass.

Everyone has a deer story to tell. Our own Robin Heillman once, in a fit of compassion, wrung the neck of a deer she hit on a highway and loaded it into her station wagon next to her sleeping children.

Because of this most recent episode and because no one seems to know exactly what is the protocol when a deer is hit (or hits us) I called the Florida Freshwater Fish and Game Commission and asked. (Remember, the only stupid question is the one that isn't voiced!) I try to be "law abiding" and sensible at the same time. Sometimes these two ideas don't jive. I get into more trouble that way.

Steven wanted to load the deer into the back of the RX-7. Steven wanted to call Harriet Smith from Rosewood. Steven would have me dressing out a dinner of venison. Steven should know that I have trouble dressing out a wild manicotti! James figured that the better part of valor was to give the deer to the closest person who drove up and looked interested.

"Did we do right, Mom?" Heck, I didn't know!

The officer at the Florida Freshwater Fish and Game Commission, located in Lake City, gave me the official prose. Then he gave me the common sense approach that I was seeking. "If the deer is dead, you may have it. If the deer is alive, you are to call this office. We will pick it up for you and see what we can do to save it."

Then came the common sense. He explained that deer rarely survive an incident with an automobile. If they do, they will immediately run away. If not, well, on a road like Highway 24 it would be pretty silly to let it decompose in this weather.

In a community that reveres its wildlife, we need to know these things. If in doubt we should call the Game Commission and report the accident. They won't repair the front or side of your car but will make you feel less guilty. And, you might have a nice dinner for months to come.

"Looney Tunes" and Other Things I Wish I'd Written
July 1991

Last week in the *Beacon* there appeared a story comparing the plight of the common loon to that of our winter visitors. (There might be some similarity, at that!) Perhaps it was because the "news release" was typographically perfect and submitted on wonderfully clean paper that the editor assumed it was written by me. (Surely, I jest!) It is more likely that because it was in a pack of "stuff" I sent in in a folder labeled "Roquemore" that it happened. Imagine my surprise then when it appeared under my byline.

In reality, I subscribe (at no cost) to "Conservation News," a newsletter of the Florida Fish and Game Commission. The information contained therein is a collection of new rules and regulations and sometimes information "stories" like the one about the loons that get stranded in Florida. It is entirely proper for the *Beacon* to run these articles *en toto*. I just felt funny about it appearing under my byline and wanted folks to know that I wish I'd written it in the first place!

My own "loon story" goes back a few years when I thought I knew something about birds. Birds are like kids: just about the time you think you know something, they move out of the neighborhood. One particular night I was driving across the Number Three Channel Bridge about 10 PM. In my path was a waddling mass of something. There was no traffic, so I pulled to the side of the road to investigate. It was obviously a bird in distress. I pulled off a layer of clothing and wrapped the bird in it and laid it on the floor of my car. Thank goodness it was a warm and dark night and I had only about a half mile until I got home. I could just see the police report if I'd been spotted: "Lady Godiva Rescues Bird!" At that time, in Cedar Key, we had a woman who regularly cared for sick or injured birds so I called her. She and a friend (not too happy about it) came to my house to retrieve the bird that I'd laid carefully under the carport, still wrapped in my shirt. (No way was that shirt going upstairs with me. Birds have bugs that even God doesn't know about.)

By the time she arrived and I had showered and replaced my top, I took her to where the bird lay. It wasn't there! The search was on! How or why this injured or tired or loony bird took off across my yard to the pile of building debris, I don't know, but in the course of the search I learned it must be a loon. The bird thought Highway 24 was a watery landing strip. Surprise! It was a loon.

I'd seen lots of loons up north on the Minnesota Boundary Waters lakes. They are shy birds, great swimmers and if you are into eerie sounds, good "singers." Never before, nor since, have I encountered one on pavement. I'm glad I didn't pass that particular guy over since I would have missed my first and only encounter with a bird-type loon up close.

That's All Folks!

Sunrise, Sunset, Cedar Key
August 1990

When I rise, she is rising. Rising in my face. Over a little clump of old dune that I call island.

Ibis cross her face to where ever the ibis go in the morning. Egrets have begun their pecking and plucking among the grasses, silhouetted as if by silkscreen created by hand.

She rises higher in the sky; the disk round, the orb nearly painful to the eye. No longer orange but a yellow-white, I lose sight of her behind the pines and clouds.

In my mind she is but a light that is warm and someplace around. I go about my merry deeds: people-things, largely.

I curse her for being so hot. I curse her for doing her work. I curse her brassiness, her glare. She is there.

Always there.

In the evening she finds her way to my back. The earth has moved, not she, but it doesn't seem that way...not here, not to me.

Her spell is cast in purples and pinks and shades of orange and blue. Spreading the Cedar Key skies with hues of sky colored spume.

The Ibis are returning from where ever they have been. The osprey are still working to feed their young their dinner. Egrets heard the dinner bell an hour ago but the mullet are still jumping.

A happy red-wing blackbird sits in the top of the most precarious limb on a cedar tree. At least, he looks happy to me. He tears away on a mission importantly.

I don't see the sun set often, but I see that she does. She's painted my world often enough.

World of the Wraparound Sun. Today's today and tomorrow's tomorrow. Thy Will be Done, Everyday, in Cedar Key.

A Picture Album

Dave atop Seahorse Light—1989

1988 Senior Class, Cedar Key School—Jimmy Allen, Steven Roquemore, Lamar Gore, Jerald Beckham

The old water tower—1988

Shadow learns to be a Cedar Key cat—1987

Gathering oysters in the No. 3 Channel—1987

Susan and a bowl of Thanksgiving oysters from the Number 3 Channel next to the picket-fence rental house on Whiddon Avenue—1987

Mack McCain was a Cedar Key treasure, the man to call on for any heavy equipment work. He promised us a driveway by Thanksgiving but we forgot to ask: "Which Thanksgiving?"—1988

The 1988 Senior Class sells clam fritters (wild quahog clams gathered by them) to help fund the Class Trip to Gatlinburg, Tennessee

Almost complete, a home on Boogie Ridge—August 1988

*The Cedar Key Garden Club lemonade stand,
the source of the troublesome white powder*

Susan and the "Green Beast" dolled up for the 1991 Christmas Parade

The Honeymoon Cottage after Hurricane Elena
Built in 1959 by the Thomas family of Gainesville and otherwise known as the Thomas Guest House, the Honeymoon Cottage suffered greatly from 1985 Hurricane Elena, which stalled just 50 miles west of the Cedar Keys.

The Fishing Pier after Hurricane Elena—1985

Dorothy Tyson and Polly Pillsbury and the Cedar Key Historical Society float for the 1991 Christmas Parade

Canoeing the Suwannee River the day before the 1993 "Storm of the Century"

Aftermath along Highway 24 of the "Storm of the Century"

Dave and Dr. John Andrews at the Atsena Otie Cemetery

The "Sharkmobile" in the 1990 Seafood Festival Parade

In The Middle Of History

*1985 Civil War Reenactment of the
Skirmish at Station No. 4 February 13, 1864*

As the Wind Blows!
February 1993

One nice thing about having this column called "Impressions" is that no one ever cites me for being historically inaccurate. My mother came closest: She chided me for a reference to finding a jar of baby teeth she had saved. I almost doubted myself—until this past week, when I found that jar of baby teeth again among her personal things! (Score one for *historical accuracy*.)

Now Cedar Key is faced with trying to find out the way things were, both in Rosewood 60 years ago and in downtown Cedar Key more than 100 years ago. It's hard enough for me to remember being curious as to why official road maps clearly showed Sumner and Rosewood at least as large as Otter Creek as late as 1985. My mind's eye is selective and memory must necessarily be inaccurate.

My first impression of the Rosewood Incident was that it was a product of the times—fear generated between races—and in no way an isolated incident unique to the rural south. This is not to condone murders, but I cannot possibly see how or why justice would be served by condemning the descendants of those accused. Even if we could find just one or two eyewitnesses who engaged in the activity—their memories would be colored (no pun intended) by their own perceptions—and probably wouldn't agree with each other. We simply will never know the whole story—as sensational as it is.

Now the ever-charming hamlet of Cedar Key is getting face-lifts right and left and some people seem to be worried that some of the restorations (or remodelings) aren't in keeping with historical accuracy and are too fancy for Cedar Key. Even with its designations as one of the few living towns on the Register of National Historic Places, Cedar Key is not a museum or buried in a time capsule. Cedar Key has a long and colorful history (and prehistory). Just which era should we choose to make the place historically accurate? Must we rip out our telephones? Our TV cable? Our electricity? Paved roads are not historically correct either.

Some of Cedar Key's finest historic homes were built between 1870 and 1900. This is what is commonly referred to as the Late Victorian Era. These homes were built by successful businessmen. Cedar Key in her heyday boasted a railroad, a deep-water port (second only to Jacksonville's in the state), a healthy economy (and no income taxes); affordable labor without the hassles of workers comp or filing all of those government forms. Why would anyone think that the builders of these homes would be less than *trendy*? In a town that shows evidence of society with *formals, informals, hops*—there was every much as rigorous social strata as those less frontierish palaces. *Trendy* in Victorian terms generally raises my hackles. Victorian to the younger generation means *Haunted Castle At Disney World*! To me, it means women wearing corsets and men who thought they were infallible. It conjures up images that I don't like. Residences—for my own personal tastes—were garish and over-ornamented. For the record, I never craved a Victorian castle. (You could give me an old cathedral, however!)

Home restoration presents an interesting quandary for those watchdogs of Cedar Key who want to keep an eye on what is happening in the historic district. If the restorers of these homes are striving for a modicum of accuracy, they need to check out other homes of the same era—especially in Gulf Coastal Florida. One such contractor in Cedar Key is doing just that. He (and the owners) have found that homes of this era were rarely plain-Janes. They were far from conservative—often employing four or five colors and some decidedly wild combinations. These were called "Painted Ladies." Depending on the owner's choice, the colors schemes can range from shades of blues and grays to scarlets and oranges to bile greens. I like to watch a house come out of the doldrums, regain new vitality. Houses smile.

With the waning of the Victorian Era, tastes changed. Don't ask me why—the Roaring Twenties should have been a time of abandon but white houses were *in*. In the Midwest, even brick buildings were painted white. No reason to disbelieve that the owners of these fine old homes didn't follow this fashion: painting out the purples and pinks, removing the gingerbread in favor of simpler, straighter lines on their homes. One thing is sure, it made it easier to paint!

The question we need to address is how much latitude do we give a restorer of a fine house and its owner in the historic district of downtown Cedar Key? Remember that these people are creating a place to live—they should be given a say in how to spend their money—within some guidelines of historical accuracy. *History* is the will-o-the-wisp—the Catch 22.

The Adventures of a Museum Buff
January 1989

I am quite at home in a museum (and make no wisecracks about my age). I like old things, like my bathrobe, husband David, and lace, but books and tools and the everyday things of yesteryear can send me into another world, bring up questions in my mind that may never be answered.

How did those women find time to tat? (Well, they didn't have a word processor to keep operating.) How tiny and careful was their stitchery, their handwriting! How elegant their attire!

I can imagine tossing one of those garments into my stacked unit with some liquid detergent and watching it spin dry. I have enough trouble keeping T-shirts from disintegrating.

A day in the Cedar Key Historical Society Museum is a walk back into these days of bustling social activity when young gentlemen wrote flowery invitations to young ladies of the town inviting them to Hops. You have no romance in your soul if you think this silly.

Still, there are things I don't understand: how did those young ladies keep those white dresses white? I can put on a pair of white chinos at noon and by one o'clock they are gray at the knees and yellow from mustard or grass stains.

The hats are another concern altogether. I haven't owned a proper hat since 1968, unless you want to count the floppy straw one I bought on a cruise ship. I'm talking a real hat, with birds and flowers and fruit and plumes, not plastic-meshed one-size-fits-all caps. Wherever did they keep them? My meager shared closet runneth over with Nikes and Reeboks. No place for veiled creations, however permanent press. *(My later membership in the Red Hat Society changed all this!)*

Museums can conjure up less appealing thoughts. While you peruse the medical instrument collection, recognize the fact that these instruments have not changed in basic design in over one hundred years. They are still basically carpenters tools. It took a lot of courage to be a surgeon in those days—and a lot of courage to be a patient. We think about the men that devoted their lives to the sick and the remedies they prescribed. Would you still call them the *good old days*?

Cedar Key is fortunate to have a representative collection of so much of the industry of the area. Donors and lenders have afforded the museum a colorful recollection of the turpentine industry, the pencil companies that provided sawn cedar for their factories in the north, railroading, Indian artifacts.

Some days I mentally don my white lace dress and pick up my imaginary parasol and board the train for a picnic in Archer. The train will arrive in time for a box lunch social and return to the Keys at sunset. *That would be a fun trip!*

Some days I'm out there with the men placing turpentine buckets on pine trees. On occasion I'm guarding Jean LaFitte's booty on Seahorse Key. I've nursed John Muir back to health. I've survived several storms. I live in Cedar Key where it is all possible.

Come and join me on these adventures of the mind and spirit. The Historical Society Museum is a living and breathing body more exciting than any Rambo flick. Most importantly, it is all about *us*.

*Historical Society on
Annual Seahorse Trek
March 1989*

Thirty
hardy members of the Cedar Key Historical Society and their guests braved a densely humidified (call that foggy) morning March 6 for the annual venture to Seahorse Key.

Laden with bug sprays, sun blocks, swim suits under sweat pants, they made their jokes: "This is my island in the fog, willed to me by my father's hand..." The Brits among the group compared it to the *moors*. Spirits were sunny if the weather wasn't.

The show began about five minutes out of Cedar Key. Henry Coulter's launch was being *escorted* by a porpoise. He (or she) had apparently met an out-board motor at an earlier time and had a recognizable jagged dorsal fin. It kept pace with the launch, diving, swooping, racing, leaping—and as if knowing, entertained both sides of the boat.

Soon this Disney-esque creature was joined by another porpoise. They flipped and dived and jumped and cavorted, sometimes in tandem. Suddenly, without a hint of direction from Studio One, porpoise No. 1 flew through the water at top speed. He left a wake. He then proceeded to flip belly-side up and backwards! He was saying goodbye.

Dorothy Tyson, Society president, was asked, "What are you going to do to top this act?" (first the fog machine, then the dolphins).

The fog was settling into a palpable mist when the group disembarked at the Marine Biology Lab's dock. Ruth Clark suggested that anyone who frowned at the weather immediately be made to walk the plank. No one frowned.

President Tyson had arranged Act III: In the brush adjacent to headquarters was a fat and happy water moccasin on display, rapt in serpentine meditation among the palmettos. No one volunteered to interview him. Neither was the group of special interest to him. He'd probably had his quota of ankles this year.

Following the path to the lighthouse, another critter—this time a nice sized rattlesnake– leaned forward to say hello. Some of the guests were thinking that Dorothy had outdone herself this time.

The lighthouse at Seahorse Key may be small and not too tall, but getting to the top with a group can be most interesting. Lesley Pike and this writer made it first. Getting down the spiral steps with burly men coming up can be something of an adventure in itself.

It was a day of hats. A veritable fashion parade of Cedar Key chapeaux. Dorothy Tyson put aside the snappy straw in favor of last year's sailor's cap with the vegetables on the front; Lesley Pike a deep Adriatic-blue plastic rain cover that would have made Hemingway proud. It also kept her head dry. Paula Freeman, a visored corduroy flat topper.

It was a day that the blankets that were usually used to keep white slacks clean while doing yoga were today used to wrap up in Indian-style to keep warm. Florida had done it again! Laura Cook, on her first trip to Seahorse with husband Tom, bemoaned the fact that there was a perfectly dry sweatshirt awaiting her at home. She said, "I came out for a day of fresh air—and I'm going to get it—if it kills me!"

There were few of last year's activities: drowsing on the sand with a book in hand; a game of cards after lunch. We instead walked the beach, marveling and wondering when and which storm since last year had uprooted old oaks and had left palm roots bare two feet above the sand.

Harriet Smith rolled her eyes skyward and inveighed the Rules of the Road when it came to picking up things from high tide levels. Harriet herself picked up a plastic Coca-Cola bottle—does that count?

Other people collected porcelain-like shells. The group carefully put the recalcitrant horseshoe crabs back into the surf. Who but someone from Cedar Key would worry about getting the two lovers back together on the right tide? Was it indeed the right tide?

The day was coming to a close because the weather had decided to make that fog a steady stream of water. The potato chips were as limp as last night's hair curl.

The group packed up its respective bean bags and headed for home. The book was not read. The picture not taken. The art work not done. It was true Cedar Keys: Florida at its most capricious, and hilarious. No apologies.

John Muir
April 1989

Once every hundred years or so there comes along a man or woman with such vision and such extraordinary ways, so out of step with the world as it stands, that only years later are his or her accomplishments recognized. John Muir was such a man.

John Muir founded the Sierra Club, that environmentalist organization whose name has become internationally synonymous with protection of nature. John has become the legendary *guru* of preservationists everywhere. He set the pace and planted the seeds of consideration for an unspoiled America, an unspoiled world—seeds that have germinated, and a few of which are beginning to bear fruit.

If we think of John Muir at all, we think of him in the setting of the California wilderness; the high Sierras with its snow-capped peaks and tall trees; the grandeur that is the Yosemite Valley. We know of his untiring fight to save his beloved Redwood trees. We know that he approached his crusade as would a religious zealot. Few of us realize what part Cedar Key played in his life—indeed, in saving his life!

John Muir by profession was a botanist whose laboratory and classroom was the entire out-of-doors. He was to plant life what Dr. Doolittle was to animals. It is safe to assume that he spoke to the ferns, argued with the brambles and embraced the oaks. He was described by a contemporary as "a man who could get lost on the city streets but could find his way thru unmapped wilderness..."

Like many young men, he had a dream. He wanted to explore the Orinoco and Amazon Valleys of South America and document the fabled flora of those jungles. Short on money, long on ambition, nerve and good will, he set out on foot, alone and unarmed, from Kentucky for the Gulf of Mexico—the west coast of Florida and Cedar Keys in September, 1867—a One-Thousand-Mile Trek! Until that time, John Muir had not been farther south than his neighboring Indiana. He promised his mother that he would not sleep on the ground. (Little did she know!)

Muir depended largely on the hospitality of war-ravaged and suspicious farmers for lodging and meals along the way. He hadn't counted on bands of displaced former slaves-turned-highwaymen. Several encounters with marauders erased some of his wide-eyed innocence. He found that the native rattlesnakes were sometimes friendlier than the native humans. He met enough hospitable Southerners to keep his body and spirit alive.

He expected that once in the Cedar Keys, he would board a vessel bound for Cuba and thence to South America; more study of his beloved flowers and plants which he described as "the smile of God." John Muir was a profoundly spiritual man.

A few days before October 23, 1867, John Muir smelled the salt in the air. Long-winged gulls met him. His mind transported him back to his native Scotland with its high bluffs and sea sprays. He was approaching the Cedar Keys. This was not Scotland! He had momentarily forgotten the magnolias and palmettoes that surrounded him. It was that relentless olfactory sense so keen in childhood that screamed "Dunbar!" "Firth!" to his mind.

Muir found himself at an empty harbor with money for passage but no vessel to board. He was feeling especially alone and none too well, having eaten little but breads for the past several weeks, drinking from murky streams and defying his mother's wishes by sleeping on the ground, sometimes with a headstone in a cemetery for a pillow.

"Should I continue down the coast to Tampa? Key West? to find a vessel?" John Muir really had no conception or respect for distances.

Muir did what any tourist today would do; he stopped in a local store and asked questions. He might have said, "I'm trying to get to Cuba. Do you know of any boats leaving?" The shop keeper probably gave him a beady-eyed stare, sized him up for a reputable, if strange, customer and shouted to his wife, "Hey, Mamie, tell this feller where the Hodgson' Mill is. Fact is, son, that the mill has a boat goin' out in a coupla weeks. Old-Man Hodgson probably needs help down there right now—he's got a load of timber due in Galveston and can probably use a strong back right now."

Whether the above dialogue actually took place is moot. The fact is that John Muir did indeed find his way to the Hodgson's timber mill and worked for them awaiting passage on their schooner to Texas. But John Muir missed that boat. John became increasingly fatigued and feverish, finally collapsing into delirium. The Hodgsons took him into their own home and nursed him with the only available means of the day—quinine and bedside manner. The malaria progressed into a complication—typhoid.

During his convalescences, John Muir learned to sail the little skiffs of the islands. He learned the local names of the wading birds, their plumage, their language. He counted the leaves on the old oaks. He described in detail the Spanish bayonet; he was enamored of the Cedar Key cactus (our prickly pear). He was fascinated by the draping Spanish moss he had met earlier in South Carolina and Georgia.

John Muir called the Cedar Keys "a clump of palms arranged like a bouquet and placed in the sea to be kept fresh."

He could not have been particularly happy here, frustrated by his illness and his inability to work, hemmed in by a sea he could not ford. It was, as one might philosophize today, "a learning experience."

Finally his boat sailed for Cuba—more tropical than any Florida isle he had experienced. John Muir continued to suffer bouts of ague from the malaria and was exasperated that he could not trek as he had done before for long hours. The island's heat took its toll as well. He abandoned his plan to go to South America. Instead he set his sights on California—by way of New York! For John Muir, New York City was the first frightening *jungle* he had seen. He was truly afraid to lose sight of his ship and make his way to the gardens of Central Park for fear he would not be able to find the wharf again! From New York he went to California. The rest is Sierra Club history.

John Muir never returned to Cedar Key. For us who revere this strong-willed Scotsman, a man who wept openly at the beauty of nature, one who chose *the lonely way*, he will always be a favorite son.

Patrick Smith, born in Mississippi, became a much loved Floridian for all seasons through his books, in particular "A Land Remembered." Read the novel to appreciate what we have lost, perhaps forever.

```
Is It Too Much Too Soon or
Too Little Too Late?
April 1990
```

Patrick

Smith is one of those rare people who looks like he's been sleeping in the passenger seat of a car all day. Indeed, in this case, he might have been. Getting to Cedar Key from anywhere requires a bit of effort and as he jokingly remarked, "No one just passes through." He looks and acts like the person you wished lived next door. Pat's wife, Iris, is every bit as approachable but she is prettier. She likes cats and despite her hostess' protests brought two in for inspection during a reception held in their honor at a local home. The cats did the inspecting, not Iris. Mr. Patrick Smith is a Nobel nominee six times; Pulitzer three times. His books: *The River is Home, The Beginning, Forever Island, Angel City, Allapattah* and *A Land Remembered.*

He visited Cedar Key as the guest of the Cedar Key Friends of the Library.

It may sound incredible until one understands Cedar Key. Mr. Smith wanted to come. He asked no speaker's fee.

This is a man who recognizes that this is one of the few places left in Florida that can be "saved." This is a man who aches for the Florida he remembers—the Florida long gone.

Folks listened. Folks laughed. Folks pined a little. These weren't all Florida people. Some were downright Yankee. They shed a tear or two. What is gone is gone, ain't it?

In the muted light of the Cedar Cove dining room with the only interruption being the rising tide, it was difficult to imagine tires squealing and sirens shouting. It was painful to recognize there was an outside world. No one wanted to believe that people paved over paradise purposely. Author Smith reminded people old enough to remember of the Miami Beach he knew as a child—a place where one could actually see the ocean from Collins Avenue.

For some of the audience it was a nostalgia trip. For others, a glimpse of Florida carefully hidden behind the curtain called progress. For others, it might have recalled days of pork-barrel politics and red-neck nostrums. Those were the days when nobody needed to be told what a *Cracker* was: Either you was or you wasn't.

Patrick Smith writes fine fiction. Unfortunately for Florida, it is all too true.

Another "Cedar Key Convert"!!

Dear Editor:

My wife Iris and I were in Cedar Key recently for me to serve as a guest lecturer for the Friends of the Library. As one who has done this now more than 1,000 times throughout Florida and other states and foreign countries, I must admit that our visit to Cedar Key was one of the most enjoyable ever, and a pleasant memory that will linger forever.

The people who attended the lecture made us feel so at home, so welcome—almost as if we were old friends who had come together after many years apart. This sort of thing is an old-time American spirit that has almost vanished today, but is alive in Cedar Key.

This was our second visit to Cedar Key, and we are enchanted even more so than ever. Both as a writer of novels about Florida and a constant participant on the literary lecture series, I have probably visited more Florida towns and cities than a 1950's traveling salesman. Thus I know Florida—and I can honestly say that Cedar Key still retains most of the Florida magic that at one time existed but today has vanished completely from many areas of this state. I hope that you retain that special magic that is Cedar Key. In the long run of all things on this earth, it will be more valuable than all the concrete spread each day.

Special thanks also to David and Susan Roquemore for the time we spent in their home prior to the lecture, meeting additional special Cedar Key people. Thank You for a magical visit to Cedar Key!

Sincerely,
Patrick Smith

Getting Outside

Susan and Steven on Seahorse Key—1989

Lettuce See Now
October 1988

My husband has taken up gardening. To understand the impact of this statement requires a basic understanding of the soil of Cedar Key. Anything that will flourish in a pure white sand laced with osprey guano will live here and thrive.

With his scientific bent of mind, he started his research. We found that we are not in North Florida. We are not in Central Florida. We found that our soil was slightly acid or neutral, our breezes had a lower salt content than other coastal communities.

The temperatures were warmer than our latitude would suggest, but too cool (considering wind-chill factor) for more southerly crops. The only sensible thing was to do container gardening.

Dave learned about container gardening from cable television. One such presentation suggested using an entire bag (forty pounds) of potting soil set in a suitable container and simply sprinkling seeds generously into the appropriate slits. It was all too simple.

We built the container from scrap cedar and pressure-treated wood. By the time he assembled the saw, the seeds were sprouting on their own. While in K-Mart, I eyed some particularly lonely tomato plants and said "Honey? Look at these poor blue-light-specials!" I sneaked in a couple of lettuce plants who appeared to be genuinely thankful for the earthy smell of our car trunk.

The next week David built several more planter boxes, ostensibly for my disenfranchised lilies that I'd been babying along for many months in a plastic bag. He violated the lily bed with radishes!

Not too long after that, we put in Chinese cabbage, several varieties of tomatoes, more radishes and pepper plants of every sort imaginable.

David was not happy with potting soil. He found a "recipe" that was a sure thing. All I had to do was find a source of forty-year-old sawdust. New sawdust (of which we have an abundance) won't do since nitrogen is leached from the soil by this new stuff. Never one to be shy about asking people where I can find forty-year-old sawdust, I found a heap and contracted with a gentleman in Chiefland to let us dig.

Dig we did. Mix sawdust to sand 2:1 and add all kinds of iron, lime and vitamins. I'm learning why farming is such an expensive business. I'm also learning why my left shoulder is in constant dis-alignment (my shoveling shoulder).

It should come as no surprise that the peppers are faring well. One little lettuce survived. The cukes and squash are literally climbing the walls.

Then we made ourselves a mini-herb garden! Since I don't recognize these things in leaf form, I was careful to keep the catnip out of this bed. Since I don't recognize these things at all, I figured why not use them all in a Sunday omelette? A friend in turn gave me two lovely cedar trees and a hibiscus, which I dare not put in the ground without expert assay.

Gardening in Cedar Key is a fun thing. I envision the lovely rosebushes and the well-tended azaleas. I see the Brussels sprouts where cacti grow. David is determined. Still, I am yet not quite sure whether I have the sweet potato pointed the right way up.

We met a man in Chiefland who grows the most beautiful persimmons, chestnuts, figs. He has espaliered citrus up his house walls.

David is into horticulture. He's learned the word "Root-tone" and following suit, I will. After all, you haven't heard about my prickly-pear jelly, have you?

Summer in the Cedar Key Garden
July 1989

Did you ever notice that those wonderful garden shows on television are always based someplace where the soil is black, the emcee has an underground irrigation system, a rotor-tiller, inflatable owls to keep the birds away and a pair of spotless gloves? Those people always find their nippers, well-oiled and sharpened and collect their produce in a basket that I would only bring out if royalty visited. Gardening over here by the Number Four bridge may never make it to PBS, but it sure is fun.

There are certain myths surrounding growing things in Cedar Key and Florida in general that I would like to dispel, once and for all. Myth #1: Nothing grows in the summer garden. It may take several seasons to figure out how to make nightshade jelly or cutworm casserole but they are hardy Florida crops during July and August. Myth #2: Never water your garden at night. Myth #3: Never water your garden during the day. Myth #4: Always make sure your garden has enough water. And finally, Myth #5: To prevent fungus, don't over-water your garden. I've chosen to do all of the above, with the exception of making the jelly and the casserole.

Far more important than water and food that I go around and supply on a demand basis are the "givens" we are given here: Moist heat and lots of it; balmy nights and scorching afternoons. My own theory is that if I look at the things that grow wild and produce, the same thing ought to happen in my garden. Sometimes it works. Those pretty little yellow flowers that cover my back yard look remarkably like black-eye pea blooms. Sure enough, my little pea patch has produced enough peas to feed a South Carolina neighborhood. I have no idea why the tomatoes refuse to set fruit in the heat since the deadly nightshade (a first cousin) is so productive. Okra reminds me of hibiscus—we know what hibiscus does in the summer (if it survived the winter). Okra grows tall and blooms like crazy. It's easy to overdose on okra in the summer if you talk to it at all. The strawberries threaten to take over the entire place; the next thing I know I'll be written up as having produced a "strangler strawberry" strain.

Gardening gives vent to my perverse nature. I was told that asparagus wouldn't grow in Florida. Not only would it not grow, if it did grow it would take several years to reach the stage where it was dinner worthy. I planted asparagus. Right now it is in its fern-like stage and very pretty. If I'd known it was going to look like that I would have put it in with the lilies and invited the neighbors in to graze.

Nobody in this house eats papaya willingly. The tree is lovely and the fruit exotic looking. One day several months ago I was admiring the trees next to the *Beacon* office. The kind owner allowed me to climb the tree and pluck a couple of the juicy fruits. That evening I valiantly tried to eat papaya. I keep trying things like mango and soursop and papaya thinking one day my palate will change, like it did with avocados. I saved the seeds from that papaya but promptly forgot about them. A few days later I smelled something in that fruit basket—a rotten papaya smell. I didn't get as far as seed flats, I put it in with the peppers, thinking to give the birds a diversion from their diet of tomatoes.

It took nearly three months but those seeds germinated all by themselves—and now I'm wondering how I can neglect them enough to reach tree stage. My friend Joan tells me papayas make a wonderful facial cream!

While Dave and I are devotees of the garden shows and have learned a lot from them, I've yet to be able to entice him to eat the concoctions on the recipe segment of the shows. Cucumber mousse must have been meant as yet another facial treatment.

One of these days I must find Henry Ford's recipe for making rubber from goldenrod. It will be goldenrod time before we know it here in Cedar Key!

Did You Ever Sit on a Cactus?
May 1991

There is no way I will show you the evidence, but I sat on a cactus. It is fairly important to me since I am not sitting on very much else since I sat on the cactus. I was being so very good—mowing the "lawn" (translated: "weeds") with our gasoline-powered scissors when I hit an obstacle—called a "rock"—and sat down. The mower automatically shut down and I sat down. No damage done, except to my derriere. Nurse that I am, I inspected the site. To do this I needed not only my glasses but a rear view mirror. I ask you: Did you ever try to tweeze those fine prickly pear springtime spines from your fanny? (David, where are you when I need you?) Living here is such a joy.

We spent last week in Orlando and Miami. The culture shock is almost as bad as sitting on a cactus. Where once the cactus roamed, asphalt reigns supreme. Grass is the real thing, blue-green and thick and well rooted. Trees are not gnarled. Flowers are hothouse hybrids. I kept imagining that the budget for the Lake Estelle overpass in Orlando might be equivalent to an entire year's allocation for beautification in Cedar Key. I might not be wrong. Miami folks were complaining about their 30-degree temperatures last winter while I was still waiting for the photographs of our big freeze of 1989 to be developed. We live life in the slow lane.

Sitting on a cactus isn't the worst thing in the world (it comes close). Stepping on a bee is probably worse, but at least a person can grab the foot and rub it without undue attention. Headaches are nice. They are voguish. Arthritic joints are fashionable. Who, pray, sits on a cactus? Me.

David came home and I promptly told him of my plight. I did show him the evidence.

"It will all work out in the end," he said.

"Good Night, David."

*Rose Gardens and Grape Arbors—
These Shall Come to Pass—
Maybe Even in My Own Yard Some Day
April 1991*

Some people get nice fashionable tennis elbows. I get "shovel hips." My good friend and experienced hole digger, Annette, called early Thursday morning: "How about digging some holes today?" It was, indeed, exactly what I had planned on doing. It was right there on my refrigerator door, "Dig Holes Today." (David had purchased six beautiful fence posts the day before and I'd borrowed a post hole digger to plant them for my grape arbor.)

I had noticed that my work always gets in the way of my play time and this morning I was destined to plant crape myrtles downtown instead. If those twenty-two suckers don't turn out big and beautiful and blooming it won't be because of the quality of those holes! Annette dug while Betty and I pleaded, probed and poked, cut, scissored and wrestled the trees from their happy marriages to their pots. We mulched and watered. We only have 29 more trees to plant.

Three weeks ago, a fit of madness overtook my normal lunacy and I suggested we plant a rose garden in front of the house. (This was undoubtedly provoked by Robin Raftis' vulgar display of her rose population in the *Beacon* office.) This tangent necessitated removing my ill-fated asparagus that produced enough proud spears for exactly one salad last year; my Jerusalem artichokes that produced enough to feed all of Israel; and enough carpet grass to bale and sell to the Four-H Clubs of Florida to raise 3,000 lb steers. It wasn't a pretty sight watching me try to climb our stairs that afternoon. Do you realize how difficult it is to get splinters out of one's navel? I did not use the shovel, but it might have helped.

Dave and I are a matched pair when it comes to impulse buying at the Home Depot Garden Shop. While I was selecting the cheaper cuts of roses that looked like they might survive the trip home, he was eyeing grape vines. I reminded him that he had indeed never promised me a rose garden but he did promise me a grape arbor (getting David to set a date for a grape arbor is akin to what I went through thirty years ago for a wedding!) He agreed to purchase one plant as a test. What I found out later was that the test would see whether it would live in its plastic wrapper long enough to get into Cedar Key soil (I use the word "soil" loosely).

On Wednesday, March 27, 1991 at approximately 3:30 PM Dave found the plans for building arbors. He said: "If you can find me six fence posts within a half hour, we will build this thing," with the stipulation that he didn't have to drive to Oregon to pick them up. (This speech reminded me of his marriage proposal as well—like let's do it before I change my mind!) Within the hour we were proud owners of locally purchased posts (it took a little longer for the wedding).

Because I was planting crape myrtles Thursday morning and Jeopardy intervened on Wednesday, I wasn't sure whether this arbor was really meant to be. I went through the check list: "Have you showered and shaved, eaten lunch, done your aerobics and the checkbook?" I'd picked up the mail thus eliminating that detour. "Do we know where the children are?" (That is not a question to ask when they are our kids' age—but habit, nonetheless.) The time was set on the oven timer. Alarms will go off if we aren't outside at 3 PM!

David doesn't set fence posts. These things could have grown into mature railroad ties before he was satisfied that the area was square. We work so well together it is almost frightening. The tape measure is about 2 feet too short. I suggest string, which allows me to run up the stairs to find the kite string that we bought in 1986 and might be anywhere from a sewing basket to a prom souvenir glass. I'm not exactly a geometry major but I've made a curtain or two and knew this thing was gee-whopper-jawed. (But then, I lived in Cedar Key for almost a year before I realized that the sun sets in the south here.)

David doesn't appreciate my approach to engineering things. I stick poles in the ground. He takes aerial photographs of the topography. To plant our lonesome and now very poor grapevine, he does a genealogical review on the Gallo Brothers. I do think that we bought something that might grow better in the Finger Lakes area of New York State. Will I tell him that? I'd better not—and if you do, we are all in trouble.

Next week, the mulberry tree but tomorrow we go—at David's suggestion—to buy more grapevines. What a wonderful idea it was to build a Grape Arbor! It's going to be so pretty!

And thank you for the rose bushes too.

Spring Has Sprung
March 1991

'Tis the type of glorious weather that can only happen in Florida in February. It's the kind of soft sunshine and gentle breeze that makes you peel the layers away as the day progresses and put them back on layer by layer at dusk. The bugs haven't decided it's spring yet so there is no slathering on of the Skin-So-Soft or bear grease. What you miss with the insect repellent you might make up in Bengay!

The other day as David was puttering with lettuce seeds and planting snow peas (for one last try), I was defoliating the brown freeze-damaged ferns and citrus. We had some struggling loquats that had survived in pots under the house and I felt sorry for them. "David, would you dig me a hole?" (My hole digging days are over. I always feel the desire to jump in when I finish.) "Sure. Where do you want it?" An hour later we had decided where to put the loquat. Right where the dead tangerine was. This necessitated digging up the tangerine. Then Dave decided if we put it there, we should move the woodpile. This woodpile could build a small house and is half heavy pressure-treated wood and half pretty cedar. It was also a ghastly mess. I suggested we put the pile next to the firewood pile under the stairs. This sounded like a good idea since it would be unobtrusive there and still handy for whatever projects Dave dreamed up (birdhouse condominiums or cat caskets).

Instead of reaching for the shovel to dig that hole, Dave went on a search of a pair (that means two) of gloves—one for each hand. I didn't realize his hands were so sensitive. He handed them to me and said: "Before we can move the woodpile we have to dig up the blackberry brambles! I'll dig, you pull." Let me tell you, blackberry thorns can go through stainless steel. My grousing was punctuated by "Don't Step on the canna lilies!" Finally, the area was cleared and the fun of moving this vicious pile reared its ugly head. Where I hadn't been stabbed before, I was now stabbed. My arms and legs looked like I'd been in a cat fight (and lost).

We then contemplated the woodpile. We sorted and stacked. To do this, however, I had to move all the gardening pots and tools, a shell collection and several bags of fertilizer. Eventually the wood was stacked and I quit! See, I'd forgotten what got this started in the first place. The sun was going down.

"Where are you going?"

"Don't you want me to dig the hole?"

"Oh, that!"

An Ooga-Ooga Horn Wouldn't Hurt This Biker
January 1989

Before
I moved to Cedar Key I envisioned myself riding my bike to the market and post office daily, waving gaily to my neighbors as I glided gracefully along the highway, a cute little knapsack on my back and my hair flying wildly in the breeze. I would become golden bronze and my muscles would become taut. I would become the envy of all those people sweating in smelly gyms and spas.

To accomplish this I first had to learn to ride one or the other of our 15-speed bicycles. My son, Steven, the most patient of my children, offered to teach me. This was going to be fun! His sense of gentlemanliness offered me the better, newer, shinier and faster of the two bikes. After all, he didn't want his mom to be seen on a scruffy bicycle!

We thought it a good idea to start these lessons in our old Orlando neighborhood, where I knew the streets. In retrospect it was also a good idea since I was going to be leaving town soon.

It was a fine day for a ride. He showed me how to mount the bicycle. "This is silly," I thought, "I know how to get on a bicycle!" First, you have to realize the crossbar is three inches higher than is safe for either sex and the seat could have been designed during the Inquisition.

Once mounted, he yelled, "Pedal!" (Oh yes, I forgot these things had only two wheels.) I found myself staring at my navel from the angle of the handlebars. "Mom! You've got to look where you're going!" (This wasn't going to be as easy as I thought.) How does one get in that position and still look up. I wondered whether my old neck brace was still around. "Now steer!" That was a mistake to tell me because so far the bike was doing fine on its own. I turned those handlebars and did a 180 degree and clutched the handlebars in fright. This was another mistake since the brakes were there. The bike stood still and I wound up in my neighbor's viburnum.

Steve had done a good job teaching me how to get on this creature. (It was taking on its own personality.) I did so obediently.

"Now just follow me and I'll go slow." He might have been

going slow but I sure wasn't. As he wheeled around a slow curve I went straight ahead. Fortunately there was a street ahead of me. I was a little afraid of flying over the handlebars again so I thought I'd just let the bike coast to a stop. Let me tell you something: 15-speed bikes don't coast to a stop. The pavement ran out and the road was three inches of plowed dirt.

I found out something else: you don't ride those skinny tired bikes through dirt. It went one way and I went the other. The ground was soft and I've never minded getting a little dirty. The bike didn't fare so well. I had to untangle it from azaleas.

We (the bike and I) were becoming like combat buddies. We didn't like each other personally but were in this thing together.

I walked him gently back to the pavement and alit once more.

Steven was waiting patiently for me back at the house: "Where did you go, Mom? Tell you what! This time you go first and I'll follow." That sounded like a good idea. I certainly wasn't going to go anywhere where I might meet a human or a car. I hadn't counted on the dog. I speeded up, which was a mistake (another one) because there was a big oak tree that divided this drive and a blind corner before we got to our house.

I wasn't going to risk zooming across the street, so I turned sharply into our driveway. In front of me were two pickup trucks and a red Torino that hadn't been there when we left. I missed them and sailed on down through the grass between the houses toward Lake Conway. I'd learned something about putting on brakes so the thing slowed down sufficiently for me to jump off into my own soft grass.

My visions of gliding gracefully down Highway 24 to the city turned more to what a headline might read: "Weird woman thinks she is Evel Knievel and attempts to jump Back Bayou on bike."

My biking days have been put on hold until I can find one with a flat wide seat, no crossbar, normal handlebars, fat tires and foot brakes.

Of Sails and Seas
August 1989

For the last six months Dave has been refurbishing our little daysailer. It's a cute little thing, bright yellow and white and looks like her name: "Sunbird." She's been sitting on her trailer perch for several years chirping to get into the water. A few years ago we were literally (and often) up to our necks in seas and sailing.

"Sunny" developed leaks and I developed a phobia about running with the wind with my head in the water. The boat sat idle until some enterprising Cedar Key people started a sailing club. Ye gods, David got the bug.

The first order of business was to research fiberglassing hulls. While other men sit around reading Playboy or watching Monday night football, David is explaining to me the fine art of patching a hull. (Are we having fun yet?) He had to identify the leaky areas which meant removing the deck, and replace it. To do this he had to go out and buy a new saw, a new drill and some sort of plywood. Dave and I make a pretty good team: I hold the How-To book while he does the work!

The fun began with the fiberglassing operation. He went to the local hardware store and came home with mystic mastics—gooey junk that goes by the name of epoxy. Cason's sells it in little vials that are strikingly like prescription medicine bottles. That stuff could really do a job on dentures, I bet. We mixed and poured and spread this stuff, racing against drying time—and raining time. I cut sheets of fiberglass fabric in an approximation of the shape of the area to be covered. It was like fitting a Halloween costume on a squirming two-year-old with your hands full of marshmallow cream, and the kid covered with feathers. We were pretty proud of our work. There was so much fiberglass in that boat that we were afraid it might sink due to the weight.

The sanding operation went smoother, once we located the goggles that were in the filing cabinet listed under "G." Dave painted his work, willing the leaves not to fall. He did paint over about a million mosquitoes. (Maybe we should rename the boat the "Mosquito Hawk.") My day of reckoning was coming. We patched sails, located shackles and were ready for a dry run—in our driveway. I was pretty certain that somebody was going to call the cops—but then, they don't come to Boogie Ridge, do they?

I, in fact, thought I looked pretty glamorous raising that mainsail on gravel under the oaks. Dave said that I sounded pretty silly screaming while the boat was still on the trailer! (He ain't heard nuthin' yet!!!)

The next weekend Dave brought me a present: a motor for the sailboat. Liz Taylor gets diamonds—I get Evinrudes. We were set for a trial run: without sail. I'm not really a proud person but Sunday afternoon at the downtown marina is no place to putt-putt around in a sailboat without a mast unless you want to wind up on the cover of Funny Farm Journal. We opted for the Number Four ramp and the waters thereabout to see if we were going to float, sink or swim.

Taking the prone position with my arm extended into the bilge we took off—slowly—on a high tide. We chugged around. The view from the cuddy cabin floor face down was one of those spectacular Cedar Key views people rarely document: remains of an Orange County wasp's nest, some sticky sawdust but hallelujah! no water! The next thing we'll have to do is go back to the books and learn sailor talk again. Dave says I already have a good start!

Canoes to You Too!
September 1989

The kayak has now largely supplanted the humble canoe in Cedar Key waters, but the canoe can't be beat for lazy exploring of deserted islands with your love and a full cooler of beer. Canoes and kayaks can be rented in Cedar Key or just bring your own.

Cedar Key is divine canoeing country; that is, unless you are looking for "white water." In that case, you'd better wait for a storm to brew. On second thought, don't even think about that.

While the sailboat is being refurbished, we've relied on the trusty canoe to get on the water. And what fun! Island hopping behind our house offers some nice bars for redfish and must be a lying-in hospital for catfish and mullet. Trout are there too. I've seen my neighbors—in their canoe—bring them in. Fishing aside, you can get to places no other boat, except those noisy airboats, can go. You slither up between the reeds. You'll get your feet muddy (but what the heck!) and explore the perimeters of the wildlife refuges. Mounds of shells, little conch types are everywhere! Were they blown up by a storm or were they a racoon's dinner?

It isn't wise to go to the interior of these islands—which is prohibited anyway—because there really are unfriendly snakes that call them home. If you're wearing shorts you won't go because of the sawgrasses. Some of the islands have little white sand beaches and you will be certain you are another Gilligan or Crusoe. Scale Key offers a deserted beach, littered only with shells and horseshoe crabs. We've taken a picnic lunch, the Skin-So-Soft, and lazed around just thinking nice thoughts for an afternoon.

If you're a novice to these waters be aware of the tides and the weather. It is all too easy to get stuck on a low tide. We've found that, for whatever scientific reasons, the bay can empty pretty fast around here. Then you'd have an interesting choice to make: wait for the tide to rise or slog through the mud to land. Our mud ain't pretty!

My memory recalls such a day:

"Jimmy! What in the world happened to the canoe?"

"Well, uh, Mom, uh, it was like there was no more water out there and we uh had to uh like uh drag the boat back in."

"Who dragged the boat back in?"

"Well, uh like Steve." (I had a keen enough eye to notice that Jim and his friend were not covered head to toe with gray gooey glop.) Since that time they believe me when I tell them to check the tide charts.

Weather is just as tricky. Don't rely on forecasts. Keep your eyes on the clouds. Storms can build up fast—but chances that you will be within easy distance of land is good.

Before you set out, have some idea where you are. Pick a landmark. Lots of folks use the water tower. We use our roofline.

Canoes are practically maintenance free. Maybe that's why ours is available when the rest of the fleet is in dry-dock for repair. All you really need for a successful and fun canoe trip is two paddles, life jackets, a big jug of water, a rod and reel (and some bait, maybe). Wear shoes and a hat. And you will need a canoe!

While you're "paddlin' Madeline home" (or vice-versa), take time to watch the mullet jump or the porpoises play out there in the bay. We even once were witnesses to a real "The Eagle Has Landed" afternoon—the eagle was busily engaged in trying to haul his much-too-large catch onward and upward to his aerie, a quiet drama in our own "backyard."

Fishing Licenses, Fines and Funny Business
December 1989

I failed to mention in this story that Dave, at the time of his "arrest," had recently filed his application for lawyerdom, in which he was required to disclose his criminal record. He dutifully reported his conviction—-without any response from the Florida Bar Association. I guess he was just not criminal enough.

The only time I can remember David ever getting into trouble with the gendarmes was when we were sitting in the middle of Little Lake Kerr in the Ocala Forest so-called "fishing" without the appropriate licenses. The only thing we had bagged that day was a good suntan. Dave was duly ticketed but because I was about eleven months pregnant the officer took mercy. I think he was afraid he might have to deliver me in the jon boat if I got upset! We paid our fine the next day and I've thought about the incident many times since. We knew we were wrong and the fine was hefty but fair. Still, we only went to the lake once or twice a year and weren't serious about fishing. Somehow, it just didn't seem right that we should have to buy the same license as the people who lived there and fished every day and actually caught fish.

Since that time we keep our Florida fishing licenses in order. It always seems a shame to me that we cannot partake of a few casts in another state in which we might be spending only a few hours. It usually takes that long to figure out the laws that govern the fishing.

Don't misunderstand: I am a firm believer in fishing and hunting licenses. The monies derived go to protect our lakes and rivers and now shorelines. It is only right that if I am going to entertain myself with a rod and reel that I should pay my fair share of the upkeep—wherever I am. Therein lies one of my questions: What is a fair share? Should the day-visitor pay the same as the resident who lives on the shoreline and fishes every weekend all year long?

Richard Bowles, a sports-fishing columnist for the Gainesville Sun (and other publications) has asked some serious questions of the DNR regarding the new rules regarding saltwater fishing licenses. While I will make light of the scenario, the questions themselves are still in need of answers.

Mr. Bowles questions the phrase which exempts fishing "from land or from structure fixed to the land," with reference to the spoil banks off Crystal River. How about the oyster bars off Cedar Key? He wants to know whether a friend can haul someone out to one of these banks to fish and bring him back when finished. Can an unlicensed person swim to one of these areas? Colonel Brown of the DNR states that those who attempt to fish from vantage points not readily accessible by walking are in violation.

The word "land" means from dry land to a water depth of four feet.

My imagination went wild.

Jimmy comes home from college a few weekends out of the year. "Mom! I'm going to take the canoe out and go fishing!"

"How deep is the water?" (I've always cautioned him not to get caught on a low tide.) "If there is more than four feet of water, you can't go!"

"Mom, will you make up your mind?"

"Stay out of the channel—it's too deep!"

"How about if I walk the canoe out and stand beside it and fish?"

"Well, I guess that might be okay. Be sure to come back on a low tide if you have any fish in the boat."

"How about if I just put a long rope on the canoe and *affix it* to land? Is an oyster bar land at low tide or is it part of the water?"

"Heck, I don't know. Why don't you just go out and spend the grocery money on a saltwater license?"

Mr. Bowles also points out some other exemptions that are certain to cause problems, especially in Cedar Key where we have a goodly number of part-time residents who are over 65 and aren't Florida residents for voting or driving purposes. They will get no benefit from the so-called exemptions. Another question: should there be any exemptions at all?

It will undoubtedly be left to the courts to interpret this jumble of phraseology. Meanwhile, some of us will simply buy licenses and other folks will just buy several thousand yards of rope, and maybe some nice tall wading boots.

Low Tide in Cedar Key
April 1989

There is something very special about living on the marshes of Waccasassa Bay. It's such an *alive* place to be. To those who just glance, it looks utterly peaceful, quiet, inert, static. "Where is the water?" they ask. They can't wait for a high tide so the flats are flooded and it looks like a bay again. It's the lows that are fascinating. There's a deliciously earthy smell of the vegetation and salt. It isn't a rank smell but something like a freshly tilled garden or the romance that accompanies the mid-westerner's feeling about new mown hay.

The birds seem especially active at low tide, collecting dinners, wading, talking bird-talk to each other. The flats reveal the tiny channels of deeper water and the larger ones where boats can and do go. Low tides allow me to walk to my little island behind my house and explore or just sit. There is a raccoon colony out there and in the early morning on a low tide you can see the family wading out for their morning fishing expedition. They also wade over to my house for fresh veggies to go with the fish!

I'm learning the lingo of the tidemasters. For some reason people won't tell you these things: the old-timers feel that one must learn on one's own. Maybe they are right. It's appreciated more to find out what a "flat tide" is when you've been trying to figure out why the water level hasn't changed much over the past 24 hours. "Voila! I think I figured out what that means."

If we are to know the excitement of the Cedar Keys we must tune into our sea. It is different from the ocean. There is no roar or splash or crashing tides that come in regularly (save the occasional storm). It is a gentle transition from high to low tide; almost beguiling. Ask my sons who wound up wading a canoe across the mud because they misjudged their timing and wound up with no water.

The bay is a quiet drama. It's easy to look out my window and think of it as a large lake for it is often placid looking. Placid like a forest is placid. It's teeming with life and activity. Dependent upon us who love her as a baby for her continued health.

The next time someone says to you (or you are tempted to say) "Where's the water?," smile that little smile to yourself and breathe in the loveliest of all sights: Low tide in Cedar Key.

Travels with Mr. Dave

The Telford Hotel, White Springs, Florida

Every Which Way but There
August 1992

"How far is it to Washington Square West? The baby is getting heavy."

"I don't know, but I'll carry him for awhile."

Dave was so sweet. He then handed me the two suitcases, the diaper bag and remains of bottled formula. I'm thinking that I said the wrong thing! We had arrived in New York City's Greenwich Village, in the best tradition of refugees, in the sizzling September of 1964. We'd made our way north on a plane bound for Newark, New Jersey, to avoid what we heard was always a congested JFK Airport. We'd found the Hudson Tubes, and then the IRT subway and surfaced in the Village.

Oh, weren't we smart? I suggested that we might well invest in a taxi since we didn't have any idea where the apartment was in relation to where we were. First child Davy, infant that he was, made the decision by doing what babies do best. In those days before Pampers, it was critical that we find our new home as soon as possible.

"Taxi!"

New York cab drivers are fabled: this man's face told us that any tip would be larger than the fare. He turned one corner and we were "home" for the next ten months.

Our "suite" was on the sixteenth floor, overlooking Washington Square Park. It was furnished with a couch, a dresser, a bed, a table, three chairs, a tiny refrigerator and a gas stove. I changed the baby and Dave went out in search of a store that had real food. We had plenty of Gerber's cereal and formula.

He came back with a subway map, a six-pack of beer, some hot dogs, and a loaf of bread and a can of tomato juice. I reminded him that we needed a can opener. Back to the store! We had to drink all the tomato juice so we had a pot to cook the hot dogs in. It had to have been 110-degrees in that apartment and no air conditioning. We opened the screenless windows and vertigo set in. I'll say this for our baby: he was very patient with his parents. I put him in a dresser drawer and he slept for the next thirteen hours! (No, I didn't close the drawer, either.)

The next day, Dave went to town and brought home a fancy

stroller, a feeding table, tons of baby gadgets, some glasses and a pot or two. He was funny enough in the elevator; I can only imagine what he looked like on the subway with all of those boxes and bags. Once I had "wheels" for the baby, I started exploring. Exploring for me meant finding a real supermarket. There was only one problem: I couldn't figure out how to get back to the apartment. Meanwhile, I found a nice dime store. We needed light bulbs. I really never thought I had a heavy southern accent until I tried to buy "lat-bubs." The clerk called for the manager to see if he could interpret. Talk about being a stranger in a strange land.

That year I learned the difference between the BMT and the IRT and the IND subway lines. While each said "4th Ave.," where I got off the BMT bore no resemblance the "4th Ave." I lived near. I spoke no Italian and was fairly sure I was going to go gray walking the sidewalks of Little Italy. I wound up buying some good pasta and fresh vegetables, snaked my way through the mews, and finally found my Washington Square Arch. Home again!

Dave never knew just how lost I was that day but was glad I found the pasta.

It is ironic that those of us born without navigational genes invariably wind up holding the map. It started when I was about five years old. In those days, my mom would let me get on the bus and go downtown alone. Tampa was still fairly insular and I knew the cops—they still walked a beat downtown. I also knew the areas to avoid and my brown oxfords could have been registered as lethal weapons. What she hadn't reckoned on was my entering Woolworth's on Tampa Street and exiting on Franklin Street on the opposite side of the store. I knew immediately that something was wrong. If there had been a *Twilight Zone* back then, I would have been sure I'd entered it. It didn't bother me a whole lot but I did wonder how I was going to get back to Sacred Heart Church, where I would catch the Florida Avenue bus. The best thing to do when confronted with such a problem is to buy a bag of candy and sit on a bench. I was halfway through the orange slices (ugh) when a policeman strolled by. He directed me to the church and thus, to the bus. I never told Mama how lost I was that day, either!

It gets very funny when two people with equal directional abilities set out to go someplace together. My sorority sister and fellow student nurse and I had to go on a field trip to Jacksonville to the Hebrew Home for the Aged. We traveled there in caravan, with Christel driving me. We performed our academic duties and then decided to go to the circus. Halfway through the circus we both got the same idea: we'd go back to Gainesville and surprise our boyfriends. We found the Interstate by some miracle. Then we realized the Interstate (unlike today) didn't go to Gainesville. We recognized a highway number. Unfortunately, this highway paralleled the railroad track and we were driving a Studebaker Lark down the track instead of the road. We fixed this in a hurry. Now on the road, instead of the track, we tooled along at a reasonable speed. We knew David and Stuart were going to have a cat when we showed up this Saturday night! I said: "Christel, did we come by way of Brunswick, Georgia? Christel! We are in Brunswick, Georgia!" We never told David or Stuart how lost we were that night either!

David, the kids and I have many miles on our odometers. I have been co-pilot and navigator ever since I ran the little English Ford into a stone hedgerow in Cornwall. I mean they did put the steering wheel on the wrong side, didn't they? He figures I do less damage with a map. Sometimes he isn't so sure.

Dave was looking for a ghost town in Nevada called "Glory Hole." He was driving a nice-sized motorhome. The kids and dog were being somewhat civilized. At least the dog was. Up the mountain we went. And up. And up. And up. The road turned into a goat path. And, of all the ridiculous things for it to do in August, it started snowing! I exercised my prerogative as mother and navigator—I started crying! David backed down the mountain. We had passed the "Glory Hole" on the way up and that is what it was: a hole in the ground! I'd gotten him there. We just didn't recognize it!

In my job as a rehab nurse I needed to go out into the boonies sometimes to find my clients. One has to have a philosophy about getting lost and not panicking. Probably the most fun I had looking for someone was in the orange groves of the Ft. Pierce area. Does anyone realize how many Ben Hill Griffin Groves there are and how many miles of paths between trees there are? I do. I think I covered them all one day a few years ago. But then, I've gotten lost going to Ocala. Somehow I would up in Williston When we first moved to Cedar Key, Steven had to show me how to get to town from Gulf Boulevard. I didn't realize until later that the very idea of street names and numbers was new to Cedar Keyans of any vintage. We were in the same boat, so to speak.

Still, Dave trusts me with the map. We were tooling around downtown Athens (Greece) one afternoon. I always take him through the heart of any town at rush hour—it is such a learning experience. He wanted to see the sunset at Acrocorinth. All the street signs are in Greek. A little thing like that doesn't bother me a whole lot. I mean after all, I know the Greek alphabet, don't I? He only had to make six passes at each street before I could get them translated. We got to Acrocorinth just as the golden orb was plopping behind the ruins. I planned it that way.

He was not nearly so happy with me in Vienna when I got him into a downtown traffic circle (the Franz Josef Girtle) that threatened to take up our entire vacation. I'd said to the lady at the Avis desk: "We want directions to Klosterneuberg." She responded, "Is that in Austria?" Obviously my pronunciation left something to be desired (just like back in New York City). My grandfather may have been Prussian and my grandmother Bavarian, but what I was speaking bore no resemblance to German of any type. She gave me yet another map and another adventure. It's much more fun getting lost with someone else. I recommend it.

A few years ago, Dave, the kids and I went sailing in the Virgin Islands. We took a sailing course and as part of our examination we had to navigate over a certain submerged rock called "Blond Rock." He and I took turns, first with the navigation and setting course, and then at the helm. I set the first course and Dave steered. One of us goofed because the rock was fifteen feet starboard. We switched positions. I was at the helm. Dave plotted the course. The rock was fifteen feet portside. Never did we find that rock! No wonder we have so much fun.

Touring Highways and Byways?
Helps To Be in Love
February 1989

My husband missed his calling: he should have been a tour director, a travel agent, or both. He can make the most humdrum trip an event, even an adventure.

You haven't gone to Gainesville until you've navigated with Dave.

About two miles east of the Number 4 Bridge begins the wildlife series: flight habits of hawks, air currents, feeding routine of the ibis. He will point out the subtle changes in the leaves of the sweet gum, the rise and fall of the water level of the roadside swales.

We move then into the historic phase: the community of Sumner. ("Where was it really?") We take a side trip to the Shiloh cemetery (to see what is happening).

Back on the road, he may pull out his 4 X 5 view camera and set it up in the middle of downtown Otter Creek. Despite what a recognized Florida newspaper recently printed, there is more to Otter Creek than a filling station or two. The reporter simply didn't have Dave to show him the *real* Otter Creek.

A few more miles and we reach Bronson. Here we select tomatoes and avocados and buy gasoline. Part of the adventure of traveling with David is that his gas gauge is always firmly planted on empty (and the gauge is working).

He then moves from "show and tell" to the treasure-hunt phase of the trip. Have you ever counted the number of yard-sale signs between Bronson and Archer? Most of these require the use of four-wheel drive and were held three weeks before. We've noticed that nobody told the dogs they were having a sale at all. It winds up being like a drive through Lion County Safari—windows rolled up with words of "Nice doggy, please don't go for the windshield like that!"

You will know you are coming into Archer when Dave starts humming a few bars of "Hey, Bo Diddley" for your entertainment. One last stop before hitting the big time traffic lights—inspection of a boat that has been on sale since Noah released the animals.

There are other ways to get to Gainesville from Cedar Key. I don't think you are ready to hear about them just yet.

On longer sojourns we try to find interesting ways to get from here to there, eschewing the interstate system when possible. It might help to have a road map that hadn't self-destructed ten years ago. No matter! Our quests are simple—find a self-service gas station that takes a Visa card; a posh inn that will allow us entry wearing Levis; and someplace to fix the car. We aren't picky. We've found some gems along the way.

I like to remember the 1916 hotel in Avon Park that is being restored by the community college: guest quarters, dorms and a family-style meal. The community has restored the lobby and dining room to its original richness. The bedrooms are still pure 1926 plus forty years. No phone, no pool, no pets. No ice bucket, no TV, and a leaky lavatory. Adventure? You bet! I was so proud of those people that I wished I could endow a whole wing. Instead, we humbly asked for a light bulb for our bedside table lamp.

David discovered the Bellaire in Clearwater. He won't take me there until I find two shoes that match. It's an other-worldly place of swank, out of another age when leisure was an occupation.

We happened on Izaak Walton's Lodge in Yankeetown on Sunday afternoon. We were as usual rather filthily casual after spending a day rooting around some woods. The waiters were in tuxedos with pink cummerbunds, the waitresses daintily attired in frilly Victorian dress. My eyes rolled upward as we were led to an inconspicuous table. (They must really need the money to let us in, I thought.) The service was cordial and the food perfection. Izaak would have been proud.

How David finds these places I don't know. He's fed me in street cafes in Cairo and Luxor, roadside stands in Mexico. We've gathered pine nuts when we couldn't find a restaurant, and once took our own day trip along a coast eating nothing but cactus pears, purslane and cheese. (I remember the beer.)

Every good travel agent thinks about accommodations for the night. My thirty-ninth birthday was spent under the stars (in the rain) in New Mexico. (It never rains in New Mexico, you say?) My thirty-seventh birthday was spent in a cave in Utah. (It rained there, too.) I've slid down slopes in a sleeping bag. I've curled up with eight other adventurers on a fellucca on the Nile and suffered the rigors of a cell on an Alaska ferry boat with three children and a mate with two cots among us. Proper tour guide that he is, Dave woke me to see the Northern Lights. I've slept in a castle or two (bathroom down the hall).

It's not where you go or how you go that counts. It's that tour guide, that travel agent that makes it all worthwhile. It helps to be in love.

You Take Me to the Nicest Places
June 1989

As mentioned many times in my musings, there is an awful lot of stuff to do in and around Cedar Key: cheap stuff, fun stuff. (David's emphasis is on the "cheap.") Now that he is spending more time here, he has more time to think of ways to keep me entertained, off the streets, and hopefully out of trouble. (I have a very bad habit of falling into the keyboard and emerging only when lightning takes out the power or I run out of ink in the printer.)

Yesterday, he came into my office and unglued my fingers from the machine and announced: "We're going to take a hike."

"Can I take the laptop with me?"

Since I had pulled the same trick on him last week (when he was buried in financial statements, wills, and trust agreements) and coerced him into picking up trash with me on State Road 24, I felt it only fair to comply. I slathered myself with Off, put on a pair of swamp-tromping shoes and prepared a canteen of ice water, and we were literally *off* into the Cedar Key Scrub. There's an obscure parking area on County Road 347, one that only Dave or an eagle-eyed ranger could find unassisted—and some of the most exotic trail leading back into the outback one could imagine. One could see just how brave other hikers were: we figured that they turned back about the place the aluminum cans stopped showing up. We played a game: the last one to pick up a piece of trash got to give the bag away (such simple joys). I soon found out that I should have brought my water wings or at least waders, but the mud was nice and gooey and the water warm, the birds were flittering about and the breeze was gentle. Perky little blue flowers peeked up from between the jeep tracks. We were Indians. We were trappers. We were kids. We giggled.

Last week Dave canoed alone. He brought me home a perfect whelk shell. The next day he took me along for ballast and showed me his *private* island. We sat there awhile, no other craft in sight, doing nothing in particular except watching some cormorants swim in formation away from us. We watched the playful and none too hungry redfish cavort all around us.

Dave has found other mysteries of this wonder-filled place. Not long ago he introduced me to a sawdust pit outside of Chiefland. With the permission of the owner, we dug sawdust all day. For real cheap thrills, everyone should visit a sawdust pit. Another time, we went on a picture-taking safari of old cemeteries. For the price of a roll of film, it was an adventure, trying to recreate the lives of the people lying there, hopefully at rest.

He dragged out the old 4x5 view camera once upon a time, with its antique film holders. We had a blockbuster of an afternoon terrorizing the residents of Otter Creek with our imposing apparatus. We were stared at as we attempted to photograph scenes up along the Suwannee River with that gosh awful big camera on tripod, sinking slowly into the murk and mire. It didn't really matter that the film was 20 years old and wouldn't develop—it was a memorable outing—if only for the mind's eye.

It's not really hard to find things to do around here if you have David's creative expertise.

For the past few months we've spent some time with our friend Roger looking at old houses. If you have a legitimate excuse (we did) to go into and inspect old architecture, it can be an utter joy: a detective process trying to figure out *who, what, when, where, and why*. You'll discover personalities emerging from those beams and floorboards and added-on rooms. Houses have personalities and it is a time-travel type of experience.

These activities are not for everyone. Some people prefer shell collecting to trash collecting. Go to the sand spit at low tide and collect and then throw the sand dollars back (except for a few souvenirs) to make more sand dollars. (How *do* they do that?) Grab a pole and sit on the Cedar Key Dock. Feed the pelicans and the mosquitoes. Take a picture, write a book, paint a painting, rent a video of a place with more hustle and bustle. If all else fails, and you can't think of anything else to do, call me. I will let you wash my dishes, do my windows and floors, play with my cats—all for free! (And it is fun—I guarantee it or your money back!)

Day Tripping Around and About
December 1989

There's one thing about living in Cedar Key. No one just drops in because they are on the way. You either aim for the Cedar Keys or you don't. At first you are lulled by the quiet, then the charm. You eat, you bask in the sunshine or fog, take some extraordinary pictures. If you live here you will know that there are a zillion things to do, most of which cannot be accomplished in a lifetime. Others, not bent on studying the underbellies of the osprey, might get antsy after a month or so. You've caught your limit of fish and eaten your fill of oysters. (How this can be done is beyond me, but I know it happens.) Even Dave and I stray from the island now and again and have found some interesting places. Just be home by nightfall to make sure the sun sets in the right place.

County maps are available at the realty companies; histories at the museum downtown. Not everyone makes day tripping an adventure as does Dave, but with a little ingenuity it can be a lot of fun. Venture up to Chiefland by way of County Road 347 and Fowlers Bluff, where they are excavating pirate treasure from the Suwannee River. Let the proprietors of the store tell you the legends of Jean LaFitte and the hapless hunters who discovered treasure in the river earlier in this century. The poor guys were chucking mud balls into the river when the last one dropped and revealed a golf-ball-sized diamond.

On the way to Fowlers Bluff you will certainly want to take a side trip (County Road 326) to Shell Mound, which is reportedly the largest Indian mound still existing in Florida. Somebody ate a lot of oysters, 'tis sure! It's spooky, especially if you have an ounce of Indian heritage. Clamber up and around the hill and think your own thoughts. It's also beautiful and buggy and a wonderful place to put in a canoe. If you have the time, and the boat and the tide is right, the islands surrounding Shell Mound are pretty exciting. Remnants of old camping havens abound on the islands and you are easily transported back in time (before aluminum cans and plastic bottles). There's a nice basic camping area at Shell Mound. Take your own water and food. You won't find a concession stand or a coke machine.

Don't forget to take the side trip to the ranger station at the Lower Suwannee Wildlife Management Refuge Main Gate. The Rangers there are ever so helpful about answering questions and they have a wealth of books regarding Florida wildlife. If you are extra special nice, they will show you a collection of wonderful NASA produced satellite maps of the area. It was the highlight of my day to see my backyard photographed by satellite. These are available for purchase in almost any size up to 36x24. I'm not advertising it, but that is David's Christmas present. (He may not get it until next July, but so what?)

Once in Chiefland (if you've read your history) you'll understand that this was where the Indian chiefs met in pow-wow at an area called Long Pond. Our excitement in Chiefland usually comes in the form of wandering the flea market, exercising our Visa Card at Wal-mart, and plowing though the old sawdust pit on the same road as the funeral home.

Going north on U.S. 19, you'll miss a lot unless you follow the garage sale signs back among the pines. Manatee Springs is a delight and at this time of the year you may very well sight manatee. There's a nice swimming area, honest to goodness picnic areas, wooden bridges, nature trails and the cost for admission is nominal. We usually go up about as far as Cross City and turn around. Suwannee is a nice diversion. It is similar in history to Cedar Key, a bit more rustic, keeping fishing its sole economic base. If you want to see Florida the way it was, you won't want to miss these west coast villages.

There are some pretty interesting little stores along the way and some restaurants that rival the hospitality of Cedar Key's own. You'll get your catfish and hushpuppies just the way you like them and watch the river roll by.

We tend to tool around a bit and day tripping has become more of an art than a science for us. Going south, rather than north, from the junction of U.S. 19 and State Road 24, we've wandered old Otter Creek. The houses and buildings are a fascinating and worthy of any artist's brush or photographer's lens. On to Gulf Hammock and down to the Waccasassa River. Again, with the canoe, this is a wild stream that looks like it came straight from a Tarzan movie. These folks rent canoes if you don't bring your own. Going upstream, in an hour or so you will meet veritable jungle. No Cheetah met us and I was a little surprised. The river is (like all our rivers) subject to tidal flow so you have to be a little careful. The big trees reached out and grabbed a hat and I ate my fill of mosquitoes in the upper reaches. Just after remarking that this looked like "gator country," one went "ker-plop" off the bank in front of us. If we had headed downstream into the Gulf of Mexico we could have been back at Cedar Key within a few hours. Group trips are arranged for overnighters along this route twice a year depending on the weather and other conditions.

Day tripping out of Cedar Key is a novelty. David invented it. We do it. He finds islands for me to explore and sand spits to play upon. We do things like take pictures of old churches and cemeteries. We record the voices in the forests. We listen to the pine whine.

To live in Cedar Key, Florida is to live in a world apart from the rest. Every now and then, we leave this island and do some day-tripping.

Adventure Doesn't Have To Include Achy-Breaky Bones, Muscles Or Credit Cards
January 1993

We were sitting there in the car at the corner of River Road and Bridge Road in White Springs, Florida, last Thursday afternoon without a thing in the world to do for a solid eighteen hours. "What do you want to do now, Boss?," I said to no one in particular. We had until the next morning to psyche ourselves for our weekend backpacking trip with the Florida Trail folks, which was the reason we were in White Springs to begin with. We'd already visited with a canoe outfitter who gave us some advice on a future trip from the Okefenokee Swamp down to Cedar Key via the Suwannee River. We'd played the "thrift shop game" and had been to the Stephen Foster State Park many times. "We can go up and camp at Suwannee River State Park or we can get a room someplace. Why not play tourist in White Springs?!"

It didn't sound like one of the more exciting things we'd ever done but then, with my head full of pollen and my nose running off my face, I wasn't objecting to life in the slow lane. Heck, we'd left the pickup at home and we even *looked* like tourists!

Tooling in and out the side streets we happened on a big old hotel that, if set in one of the pricey New England hamlets, would have meant immediate bankruptcy to register. The architecture is just plain weird: a combination of rock and red brick trim and painted wood. It stood three stories tall and there was an obviously brand-new addition in raw cedar. It looked like it had started out being Victorian and had progressed, not too happily, into the 1990s. We loved the looks for its unabashed ugliness. The big satellite dishes surrounding the place gave it the mien of a nine-year-old wearing eyeshadow. "Well, we know it has television." The sprawling front porch had resident cats sitting or lying in various stages of repose, yawning or stretching in and about the rocking chairs and potted plants. "Let's see what it costs." (High Drama!)

Even after traveling with me for yea many years, Dave is still unsure how I am going to react to anything except an EconoLodge ("It's a port in a storm, isn't it?") or a trail shelter ("How far do I have to walk to the privy?") He recalls my not batting an eyelash at having the room with a view of donkeys and garbage cans in Cairo but refusing to stay in a room in the good ole USA where the bathtub had mold in the grouting.

I tried to read his face as he returned from his reconnaissance mission.

"It's an Island Hotel experience."

"How much of an experience?" (By this, I meant how many tent-sites could we buy for the pleasure.)

"Come look."

I stopped to talk to a couple of cats along the way to the big screen doors.

Inside is all polished old wood. The first thing that caught my eye (and ear) were the people sitting on grand overstuffed davenports listening to the radio. Bookcases act as a room divider. Dave had already been given *carte blanche* to show me around and he took me to an available downstairs room.

"How far do I have to walk to the bathroom?" (I'm a veteran of boarding houses after last summer—and this is an important issue.)

There were several upstairs rooms vacant, so we climbed the broad uncarpeted steps and followed directions to Rooms Six, Seven and Nine. Such decisions! "Nine" was a corner room nearest the fire escape. I didn't care for the pattern of the linens. "Six" was okay but too close to the stairs. "Seven" had a freshly drycleaned robe hanging there for use for me to walk straight across the hall to the old fashioned bathroom. Two old iron beds—a double and a youth bed—were in chintz. The floors were painted a ghastly porch green without a thought of a rug—and the little portable color TV with its EconoLodge remote control was just the right touch to set off this room.

"Okay?"

"Seven, it is!"

Before setting off to *tour* White Springs, we inquired about dining room hours. Are there really civilized people who eat dinner at 5:00 PM? We waved at the man in the glass-enclosed *cage* and he nodded back. This man had lived in Cedar Key for quite a few years, broadcasting a radio program via satellite to all points of the world, and it was then that it occurred to me that we were staying in the global headquarters of that "arch-conservative" Chuck Harder. Dear Me! What will my Sierra Club friends think? There is, in one of the downstairs office rooms, a "Chuck Harder Library and Bookstore." Here you can buy all manner of tee-shirts, banners, books. I expected to see fringed satin pillows (a la World War II) proclaiming doom. Across the hall I found myself lost in another world: the world of old radios. The collection is extensive and nostalgia-producing. I am a collector of old things radio. My collection is sparer but finer. (I don't have an entire hotel to display my wares.) The centerpiece of the room is a pool table.

"Wanna shoot some pool?"

"C'mon, let's take a walk."

It's fairly certain that we chose the path less-traveled. We strolled into areas that few tourists ever go. Kids hopped off their bikes to say hello. Dogs growled and voices shouted, "Start up, Bubba!" We giggled as only Dave and I do as I tortured him with a sprig of mistletoe that I plucked from a head-high branch of an overhanging oak tree. I was fascinated by three youngsters intent on some game of digging dirt from under a sidewalk. The sidewalks themselves were works of art: cement overlaying old brick. The town of White Springs is a sad old Florida town, like many Florida towns that no one ever really stops to look at. On one of the back streets an old wide porch was laden end-to-end with firewood. Smoke curled from the chimney. Work clothes and underwear hung on a line behind the house. Flowers bloomed in the dooryard. Dave and I both were lost in the reverie of our childhoods, when there were black iron pots in the backyards. Across the street was a burned-out shell of a frame structure: charred mattresses laying hither and thither and twisted melted toys among the rubble. Next to the horror was a real mansion in the process of being renovated: a spanking new fence that spelled "swimming pool" to my eyes. Sure enough, I saw it between the cracks of the boards. Nice pool. Whoever was doing the renovation of the big house hadn't cared enough to scrape the wood before painting. We mused: "That paint won't last long."

We'd been walking for more than an hour and dark was setting in. We'd taken a couple of pictures, just like tourists are supposed to do. Dave tried to catch me as I spoke to one of the resident cats. We hauled our *luggage* (plastic bags-full) up the stairs to "Seven."

I was rapt in a TV movie: *Reptile,* when there came a knock at the door.

"I'm your next door neighbor and I was wondering if my TV was bothering you."

I turned *Reptile* down to a murmur. Whether he was sincere in his query or just being polite, I will never know, but it is the way in old hotels to be genteel. It brings out the politeness in us, the suaver side—a side lost next to the ice machine at the Holiday Inn.

Our next *walk* was to the Hometown Cafe about 7:00 PM. They closed at 8 o'clock. The cafe was a stereotype of so many places we choose for breakfast. At breakfast, the men are dressed in their jeans and tees and jackets with caps that read "Red Man" and "Caterpillar." They are slugging down the coffee. They're always a little disgruntled. At dinner, they bring the wives holding babies in carriers. They order the all-you-can-eat mullet dinner and get their money's worth. It must be an unsaid rule that no one ever smiles in a hometown cafe if you are a hometowner. Since we were tourists we smiled. The waitress understood and forgave us our transgression. We traipsed back down the lighted alley that looked all the world like somebody's backyard with Christmas lights strung. The cats greeted us. Coffee was brewing on the sideboard.

There's not much to do in White Springs, Florida. Who really cares? For twenty-nine dollars, it sure beats playing in the traffic!

Hip-Hip-Hippodrome
June 1990

"How old are you really, Mom?"

Those are words that strike terror into the hearts of any of us who have children old enough to utter them. Over the years I've learned some cutesy answers and use them, unless father beats me to the punch line.

"Son, your mother remembers the three-cent stamp."

The poor child pulls out the chair and covers my knees with a lap robe.

"Why, I'll bet you she even remembers home-delivery ice trucks and chomping on slivers of ice that fell off the truck."

"You really did *that*?"

I smile benignly and give father one big kick in the shins. "Yes, but I was only fourteen months old at the time."

"How old are you really?"

As I learned in Psych 101, always answer a question with a question. It is called "reflection" (should have been called deflection). "How old do you think I am?" (Here, I am hoping they never read my birth certificate, and if they did, proved their mathematical prowess by subtracting rather than adding years.)

No such luck—out comes the calculator. Fortunately, it is solar-powered and its a rainy day. "Dearie, let me tell you how old I am. I mailed letters from the Hippodrome."

"Aw, C'mon. Nobody's *that* old."

I hadn't been in that building in nearly thirty years. I was using a three-cent stamp to mail a letter. Why or how I wound up at the marvelous old post office in downtown Gainesville, I don't know. In those days they shot students on sight. Maybe I didn't look or act like a student.

As a family, we went to a play last Sunday at the Hippodrome. The fact that the play was good was a bonus. I fingered all the brass except for the doorsills. I stared at the marble entrance ways, gently eroded by zillions of feet that carried hands mailing letters: one pair were mine once upon a time.

I never got into the recesses of the post office and only vaguely remember where I bought the stamp.

Today's Hippodrome is much more of a marvel than is the memory. Beginning with the people who sell tickets, the entire experience is one of graciousness. I'm not bashful about asking for student or senior citizen discounts: these were not applicable for this performance and denial was accomplished by a lady who could have been Anne Boleyn's hairdresser. Once inside there is a remnant of a bygone era: the elevator operator who operates an elevator. It has a grille. It has outside doors. It goes up and down. Folks with problems with stairs may ride. Nobody needs a sticker on his or her forehead. It was refreshing to see that somebody allows a non-card-carrying pregnant woman "handicapped" status.

The theater itself is a joy. Only twice before have I felt as much a part of the set. First in Vienna when the circus elephants spewed me with water. Another time in Manhattan, for a performance of *The Fantasticks*. El Gallo spat on me—by mistake, I think. Whatever the post office used this room for, I cannot imagine, but it could not have been a nicer, more elegant stage.

Driving Miss Daisy could not have been more appropriate. Son Steven gently maneuvered his grandma into her seat next to his and in a row or so behind us. Once we heard her chuckle, "She's in worse shape than I am." The actress would be proud.

Gainesville should be proud of the Hippodrome. We should be ashamed for not having visited her sooner.

My Life In Cedar Key Time

Wonderful Ideas (That Didn't Work!)
April 1993

If you've ever had the dream of building the perfect house, hope that it is just a 24-hour virus, take two aspirin and call me in the morning. Even if you have the creativity of a Frank Lloyd Wright and the money of a sheik of Araby, I assure you that there is no such thing as either the perfect tent site or the perfect palace.

We designed our house with the help of an architect. We still don't have a place to put garbage in the kitchen. We use *decorator* plastic bags on doorknobs—which work just fine but drive our eldest son to distraction. (He uses plastic bags on cabinet handles—but that is okay for him; he didn't design his house!)

"Mom, you could just cut away this cabinet, put shelves over the counter, rip up the tile work and put in a lazy Susan."

"A 'What?' did you say?"

"It would probably only cost a couple of thousand dollars and then you'd have a place for a garbage can."

What we use as a dining room was meant to be a sunny porch for houseplants. The table and four chairs there now accommodate my two cats nicely. Occasionally, we invite two other people to share our table.

Our many odd-shaped windows are a source of pride to us. Ignore the fact that the sun bleaches everything to a chic ecru. Sit too long in my living room and you'll either be bleached or sunburned. I refuse to have curtains or blinds on these wonderful windows. The thought did occur to me after this recent storm, since now the glass is crusty with salt. Dave had only recently invented a way to clean those prow windowsills of cobwebs. (How he found a crayon up there I'll not even wonder.) He hangs over the loft with a 25-foot pole onto which is attached a work glove sprayed with Endust. It would make a wonderful Funniest Home Video as the white glove dances overhead raining debris from the ceiling sky.

It is not the house's problem that those carefully designed guest rooms (each with a full-sized closet) now each has a full computer rig and sound system. Where guests were supposed to hang a bathrobe and a change of clothes is now floor to ceiling boxes of *things we cannot live without*. That handy downstairs closet (that I lived without for seventeen years in a 22-room house) now holds everything from shotguns to fishing gear to my birth certificate. The linen closet houses my collection of crock pots and coffee grinders, blenders and fryers and broilers.

Probably the most frustrating thing for me has been doors. We planned the house correctly but some time between the blueprints and the building we had to move the house around on the site to make the septic tank people happy. This put my front door way off to the side and my back door in front of the driveway. The humiliation I've experienced over the past five years cannot be measured in words. Princes and paupers alike wade past the cats' drive-thru window, over the rattlesnake blood stained steps, past my recycling and composting projects to my kitchen door. If they make it that far we are old friends. They can read all of my window stickers while I am trying to figure out which doorbell rang. I keep hoping someone will eventually find my front steps.

Having three sets of steps up and down is another manifestation of the builder's nightmare. The waterside section was supposed to end in a patio area. Somehow it just *ends*—thrusting the unsuspecting stair-user into blackberry brambles. A nice touch, that—it is something of a Zork phenomenon. (You've lost all your points, go back and look for the front door again!)

Like most people who build houses from scratch, Dave and I pored over magazines. My dad insisted we incorporate plans for an elevator (we did). ("Susie, you are not always going to be so frisky!") We didn't build the elevator, but we thought a pulley system for groceries would be helpful. What a joke! Besides the fact that the pulley and basket were on the opposite side of the house from the car-bay (in the middle of the blackberry brambles)—which meant I'd have to haul the bags to it, then run up the stairs and haul them up and run down again for the second and third bag—the pulley blew off in the first wind. I manage nicely with grocery bags slung around my neck and on both arms.

Probably our greatest misconception about living in Cedar Key was that I'd go into the big city at least once a week to do shopping. After living here six years, full time, the big city offers me nothing more than Walmart, a dentist and a doctor. (Of my many addictions, shopping ranks last!) This translated means that I do not have to buy foodstuffs or supplies in quantity—except for cat food. This meant that the specially designed pantry could be used for plant food or bulbs or something equally important.

I am not a novice when it comes to Florida gardening. I hang my head in abject shame at what I don't know about Cedar Key gardening. My sun porch gives me dried ferns; my deck treats me to sere vines and salty lemons. The carefully designed planters where I was going to grow cut flowers now are full of fecund aloe and cactus. They bloom happily. It was not in the plan to grow cactus and corner the market on aloe vera.

Cedar Key does that to a person. You don't argue with her.

Just as there is no perfect house, there is no perfect place. Insist on doing it your way and you will be disappointed in Cedar Key.

Just a month or so ago Dave and I were bemoaning the need for a utility shed and he and I really do want a dock someday. My brown eyes turned green as I saw neighbors put up the new docks.

Losing docks to storms is part of coastal living: "If God had meant docks to be there...etc, etc..." I couldn't help but be glad we didn't have one to lose. We never learn. We will build a dock someday. A big wind will blow it down someday. That is part of living here. There are no perfect houses or perfect places.

Some ideas work...and some don't.

We eventually built the dock. It hasn't blown away. Knock on pressure-treated wood!

When the Merry-Go-Round (and Everything Else) Broke Down
September 1993

There are some days (and weeks) when ya' shoulda' stood in bed. I, who have come to espouse the simpler way of life, was put to the test. When, on the first Monday home from the Trail *(our first completion of the Appalachian Trail)* my car didn't start, I wasn't really surprised. It really didn't bother me much at all since I had two options: I could walk to town (which was the plan anyway) or I could call Lester, the taxi-man. I walked on Monday and called Lester on Tuesday. By Wednesday the car still wasn't working, but Dave was here to do the town thing. We walked, despite the fact that his vehicle ran perfectly well. By this time the dishwasher refused to wash. That was okay since I'd gotten my cooking and eating routine down to one pot, one bowl and one spoon. Even I could manage that. But now, the phone wasn't working either. The phone got fixed (for the day) but the dishwasher didn't, despite some valiant efforts on the part of the repairman. (It took me many tries to call our serviceman before someone informed me that Chiefland is not a local call.) Not to worry! About this time the washer refused to spin. My clothes literally became drip-dry garments hanging from the deck. The washer fixed itself (maybe it was just wanted attention). I did remind it that the repairman was coming back anyway and would get it good if it didn't start spinning. It spun.

It started raining in the late afternoon, precluding my walk into town. I decided to call Lester again—the phone wasn't working again.

Dave called from the hinterlands (how he got through is a mystery) and this served to deceive me into thinking it really was working (which it wasn't and had no intention of doing). Neither would the car start. Neither could the repairman call me to tell me when he was coming to fix the other things. Neither could I call and harass the upholsterer who has had my furniture since April. (Not that I was in a hurry to get it back, because then I would have to put everything back in all those drawers!)

I'd especially been avoiding my computer keyboard. I'd dismantled everything before we left town (and hidden all of my disks in case I didn't come home). If there is one thing that doesn't work, even when everything else does, it is my computer. I already knew that the printer had died last spring. There was no use trying to write anything longhand either. Glutton for punishment that I am, I plugged it all in. I got the familiar "Disk Error Reading Drive B" which means that no matter how many times I "Retry or Cancel," it isn't going to work until it feels like it.

"Okay Buddy, I lived without you all summer, I can wait another few days, weeks or months."

In fiddling with all of my plug-ins, I messed up the clocks and spent the day resetting them. (Who really cares anyway?) It's probably a good thing that I don't watch daytime TV, because by the time the weekend rolled around it was about the only thing still working in the house. Long ago, I learned not to hit Dave with all the broken appliances at once. It's hard not to, when the first thing he reaches for upon entering the house is the phone. "Errrr. It doesn't work."

Why he had to pick it up and say "It's dead" is beyond me. Then I began my litany. We spent the next day reporting things and he proceeded to charge a battery, talk to Drive B, get a printer operational and complete an income tax return. He went to his truck to drive to the Post Office. Flashing lights told him to "Get thee to a mechanic." (And it's not even a Full Moon!)

The Light of My Life

This morning I awakened to the glorious sun streaming in the east windows, directly into the bedroom and thus my eyes. The goddess of dawn was demanding I pay her some attention. Another little goddess was telling me it was Tender-Vittles Time. Nothing to do but rise and shine. The clock registered 6:55. In five minutes it still registered 6:55. Hey Now! Unless I'm caught in some peculiar Cedar Key time warp, that clock should be moving its hands. (At least it wasn't blinking 8's at me like the one in the kitchen does periodically.)

The kitchen confirmed my suspicions that we had no power in the house. My first thought was, "Did David pay the electric bill?" I dismissed this thought first of all because it was seditious but also because I just couldn't imagine any electric man so dedicated as to come to Cedar Key in the wee hours of a chilly morning just to persecute me. My paranoia has not reached that level yet.

Steve rolled over in his bed and groaned: "Did you check the breakers?" I checked the breakers, but a lot of good that did me since I didn't have my glasses. Have you ever noticed how much alike "Off" and "On" look when your glasses are one flight up and your eyes are on the first floor in a dark room? They were all pointing the same way so I assumed that meant they were all "On." (I have won prizes for logic and deductive reasoning—I think one of them was called The Lucille Ball Prize for Creative Engineering.)

The power was still off and I mentally inventoried the food in the refrigerator and freezer. The refrigerator section didn't worry me. Apple juice, beer, cheese and Coca-Cola have been known to survive millenia without refrigeration. We would have to drink the milk. But, sayeth I, what am I going to do with ten pounds of frozen chicken, hamburger and assorted casseroles and sauces? I imagined myself cooking all day. But no, my gas stove has electric ignition. Even more far fetched was imagining Steve cooking over the gas grill with the temperature hovering around 40. Steve's devoted but I am realistic when it comes to his magnanimity. ("Mom! You've got to be kidding!")

Oh well, I'll worry about this later. If it doesn't come back on, I'll call the electric company. Newspapers don't take electricity. And, so far I haven't had to plug the Audi in. Just too bad if I can't wash the dishes or do the laundry or write a report today. If the power outage lasts long enough, I won't be subjected to Oprah or Judge Wapner. But, Oh Dear!—what about my daily *fix* of *Jeopardy*?

About this time the heater kicked on and the familiar little green 8's started blinking on the stove. The idea of a day of roughing it flitted away as I marched toward the washing machine, leaving a trail of dirty socks (that could have waited till tomorrow).

It's a Lost Cause—
Losing the Right Stuff
December 1988

My son, Steven, wrote me from college last week to ask, "Mom, do you have my flour?" I wrote him back, "Do you have the stapler?"

Inanimate objects have a way of taking a walk on their own now and then. I have visions of a set of crystal tumblers, a pencil sharpener, a sack of flour and a stapler huddled together in the back of a closet snickering at me. This group meets with the ten dinner plates, a rope belt and a silver earring now and then to compare notes on where to turn up. "I get the refrigerator," says the stapler. Reading glasses have a more independent nature and are rarely found at all, but one such pair was discovered in the helmet portion of a Gator football lamp.

In days past, this didn't bother me too much. I simply blamed it on the children and didn't worry about the amount of aluminum in my food. Now the children, miles away, are blaming me for losing their flour!

You would think that a general house cleaning would ferret out all these miscreants. Wrong! House cleaning only serves to locate things you didn't know were missing at all—like forty-four guitar picks, twelve dozen earring backs (sans earrings), and a loaf of penicillin (right next to the stapler in the fridge).

The things I try to lose, like telephone bills, turn up on my husband's desk regularly. Bank statements, carefully hidden, emerge glowing in the night over his head.

My friend Joan once claimed she had gremlins, whimsical critters who liked to play tricks on her. I told her she was just getting senile like the rest of us. She rode around town with an antigremlin in her car. It is true that she didn't lose her car once after that. Where the stuffed animal went is anybody's guess.

Some things turn up in my house that I've never seen before. I have a lovely ladle that none of my relatives claim and a pair of size-44 swim trunks. There are towels that are inscribed with various Hilton logos and socks that defy description—one, a kneehigh fuschia color. Did these things get traded for Dave's fileting knife or the electrical connectors or the garlic press? Did this conspiracy occur in the kitchen while we slept?

The next time you watch R2-D2 tooling around, would you ask him where he put my vacuum cleaner bags? Go ahead and ask him about Steve's flour while you have his attention.

Oops...I Just Had It!

Did you ever get a traffic ticket? It is humiliating at best. At its worst, you are guilty of the offense as well.

I stared at my license tag in disbelief when the officer cited me for an expired tag. I knew full well that I'd purchased that sticker: it was one of my birthday presents.

I was provoked that I couldn't get a tag that said Levy County on it. I remember saying "David, don't let me forget where I put this thing." We tooled into the Bronson Courthouse about five minutes before closing on a Friday afternoon, admittedly a day or so after my birthday. I knew I had it, but try and tell that to the officer with the blue light.

The contents of my purse dumped onto the seat beside me, I said "Aha!" and handed him my registration and the remains of a sticker.

"Ma'am, this is last year's registration," he said. I then emptied the contents of the glove compartment. I'd been so good as to get a Levy County driver's license and thought that pink slip was it. It wasn't. I got my ticket.

Since I was only about a half mile from home, I didn't have long to fret before I took the entire car apart looking for either the sticker or my registration. Then I took my purse apart. Neither culprit appeared.

Dave arrived home shortly and I proceeded to take his car apart. He was duly annoyed with me for my transgression but was a witness to the fact that I'd purchased a tag since it was on his checkbook. This was a holiday weekend and I knew that I'd have to wait until Monday to call the courthouse. I carried my citation everywhere with me so as to prove I had thirty days to show a valid license plate.

I was sitting in the Scotty's parking lot in Gainesville when I said to myself, "It is in that purse!" Eureka! It was! When we got home I started looking for the citation. Everyone had seen it and I'd been scolded by my children and in-laws for such carelessness. Nobody doubted that it existed. But where was it?

Now I began going through the garbage of a Thanksgiving Day looking for two slips of paper that looked like receipts from K-Mart. Finally, I found both, folded neatly in my wallet. I determined to call Bronson first thing Monday morning.

Monday came and I did. The lady in charge was out of the office. Would I call back tomorrow? Yes, if I can find the telephone! Heaven help me if it gets into my purse. *(In these days of cell phones, I still won't carry my phone in my purse.)*

Spring Cleaning Can Be Traumatic
March 1989

People do a lot of talking nowadays about Comfort Foods—chicken soup, hot toast with butter and cinnamon, cocoa. There are some other comfort items besides foods.

Husband Dave has an old wool sweater that was used as moth bait ten years ago. It doesn't take a genius to gauge his mood when he wears this sweater in July.

I have pair of slippers (that is a generous name for them). They were ugly as sin when I bought them and haven't improved with age. They are two sizes too wide and an inch too long. They look like worn out fruit-boots. Once, they had a fleecy lining. Once, the suede on the outside wasn't shiny. They are unwashable, non-dry cleanable. I put them on in September and take them off in April and drag them out every time my psyche needs stroking. This says something about the location of my psyche.

Try as I might, there are certain items that I just cannot throw away. Goodwill doesn't want them. The Salvation Army couldn't foist them on a naked person in a snowstorm.

No matter how many pretty new bathrobes I've purchased or been given since then, there will never be one like my old red one that I misguidedly disposed of ten years ago. I won't repeat that error. That bathrobe has entered a hall of fame. It was warm but not hot. The sleeves didn't drag in the dishwater. It covered my ankles but I didn't trip on it. It was dark enough not to show a coffee stain or two. It was zippered low enough to be comfortably sexy when appropriate and high enough to answer the door. They don't make robes like that anymore!

The problem with cleaning out closets is that clothes take on sentimental attachments. My wedding gown has been hermetically sealed in a black and white box for over twenty-five years. Every time Dave shifts it around, he says: "Why don't you get rid of this clutter?" ("Well," says I, "I never know when I might need it again!")

We have an assortment of boots! Light hiking boots, mountaineering boots, cowboy boots. Each has been contoured to individual bunions and arches. Even though I doubt I'll be invited to the Bush's place in Texas for a barbecue, there's no way I'll part with those cowboy boots! It took all of Dallas to fit me, and once on my feet I didn't take them off until I reached Orlando. The reason I didn't take them off is because I could not get them off. Dave pulled and twisted until I was two inches taller. I know why cowboys die with their boots on (and are buried thus).

Sneakers are something else: Each pair has its own history. There are the ones that I bought for exercise class in 1978; the ones I went clamming in Alaska in; the ones with the half shoelace that my ill-fated dachshund ate. (The dog died in 1983.) Heck, I won't get rid of these things—I'd sooner bronze them!

We must have forty-seven visored caps bearing inscriptions of everything from survival courses to posh resorts. Each holds a warm place in our hearts and on our heads. Dave methodically pares down the cap supply when we go boating. He has donated one each trip to some wild river or sea, lake or lagoon. I have considered putting a band of Velcro on his head to hold these hats on since he rejected my suggestion of super glue.

Closet arranging in this clime can take on the proportions of a major organizational feat. Just about the time you think it is time to fold and bag sweaters and wool skirts (and have done so the weekend before), the temperature plummets.

Stack those shorts and halter tops where you can reach one of each fresh each morning and you will be looking for where you stashed the sweatsuits. Once the down jackets are relegated to the back bedrooms, Dave will undoubtedly suggest a camping trip in the Northwest Territories.

Cleaning out a closet takes a lot of nerve. Fortunately, I keep the logoed T-shirts in the dresser drawer. I won't have to look at them for another couple of weeks. When I finally make it to the General Judgment, I fully expect my life to flash before my eyes in the forms of T-shirts, sneakers, caps, jacket patches, gowns worn once and old bathrobes, all old friends—still happily residing in my closet.

Can This Room Be Saved?
October 1990

Every house has at least one. Why, Lord, is it always mine? The room that refuses to clean itself or allow anyone else to do it?

When I was a very young child (I'm now a very old child), I shared a room with a dining room table, six chairs and four thousand comic books, two parakeets, a cat and dog, and a space heater. That's the most orderly my room has been in the last forty years. It's a certain magnetism in my personality that attracts clutter. It's not that I like working in the middle of a mess—around me, it just happens to be there.

My father once wailed: "I thought girls were supposed to be neat!" (He'd survived my brothers' room and was chagrined.) My sister and I were not the epitome of feminine daintiness. Kathy brought with her, to our shared room, cages of hamsters who strewed seeds around like we wish the Department of Transportation would on the shoulders of State Road 24. Despite the difference in our ages (that we never thought about), we had certain things in common: we were both slobs. It wasn't that we weren't clean slobs—if ever anyone needed a towel, he or she could find a slightly damp (or moldy) one on or under our bed. By the time her hamsters has another litter, I'd opened six more bottles of nail polish and left them uncapped.

Eventually, I went away to college to room with a tidy person, (I thought.) Carol Ann didn't bring her hamsters with her but she had a habit of leaving lingerie in strange places—like in the clothes hamper. I soon broke her of that habit, I taught her how one could iron only collars of cotton shirts, wear a sweater over it, and look neat. Her mother was appalled the first time she saw Carol Ann wearing dirty white sneakers with a Villager dress. (Does anyone remember Villager dresses—the de rigueur of the early sixties?) There was hope for Carol Ann.

Once, before I moved into the university milieu, my mom had to be away for several weeks. My dad and I were batching it. I'd brought a friend home for the afternoon. Emily asked naively: "Are you all moving out or moving in?" She had seen my room.

Not much else has changed. I've yearned for one of those houses that is self cleaning. One of those places where the brass is always gleaming and dust doesn't accumulate on tops of door frames. It would be a house—or room—where spiders don't build webs and cats don't give up hair balls to the carpet, where dishes are always rinsed and stacked and the black iron skillets are seasoned to perfection. It's a place where the flowers in the quaint pot are not perennially a dried arrangement.

Some people trade cars when ashtrays get dirty, I understand. If that is so, I am in need of not only a new car but a new house. My room—consisting of 100 square feet—resists every attempt of mine to pick up the papers, organize the files or make it beautiful. I've put an antique quilt on a brass day-bed. I've decorated windowsills with cutesy plants and shells. The nice furniture is shelved with good reference books and the carpet is luxurious by my standards. Susan's *playroom* also has a half-can of peanuts, four or five cups and glasses half filled with congealing liquid, an Early Sears mirror pasted with notices of meetings tacked up with Early K-Mart tape. My grandmother's carefully quilted coverlet is decked with papers from every "Save The..." organization in the United States and abroad. Calendars, notices of meetings, personal letters each have a separate file heading. Data is filed on the floor or the bed or under a cat. It is simply of no use to put it in the metal cabinet: I'd never find it.

I'm the kind of person who calls her child long distance to find out what his area code is. To make me feel worse, he tells me.

I have a child who takes after me. I won't say which one, but he will recognize himself and someday a wife will curse me for the legacy. He arranges his clothes on the floor. Diet Coke bottles grow from the curtain rods and glasses clone themselves on windowsills.

It can't be easy being a neat person. It must be impossible to be a neat room given these circumstances.

Now, well, then, there, anyone can reform! Today I mailed my Christmas Cards—okay, they were 1988's. Tomorrow, I'll get that letter off to my mom. Jim's birthday was only last February, maybe he won't notice that the card that was sent him was lost in the morass. Tomorrow I will clean this room. Garden Club stuff goes here and letters will be mailed. Woman's Club stuff goes there. I promise to answer phone calls. I'll finish articles for the papers before saving and losing them sets in.

I'll dust and I'll clean. If you don't hear from me for the next few weeks you will know why: I've lost myself in a room of no return.

Dirt Just Happens
August 1990

How so much dirt finds its way up all these stairs and into everything including my closet carpet—where ostensibly only clean clothes lay around—I don't know. This weekend Dave and I rented a rug shampooer. The reason for this was that I was dreaming up ways to keep him off the garage sale circuit and also I was afraid I was contributing to the destruction of the ozone layer by purchasing all those aerosol cans of "Spot Out." (The spots were getting bigger than the oriental floral design in the carpet.)

It was a fortuitous weekend to rent a rug cleaner. I didn't have to haul the thing upstairs. Two grown men grunted and groaned and took out chiropractic insurance. They then put me behind the machine. This particular model isn't as cute as R2-D2 but has the same personality.

He (it has to be masculine) comes with a Dopp kit of hoses, connectors and plugs. (It's like when I go to the beach for a weekend.) They brought it to the first level of the house and took a half-hour break that lasted the rest of the day.

I said "David, I really cannot figure out how to get this thing put together."

"Susan, you've been doing this for the last 25 years; how could you forget?"

"It's easy—you are home!" (I wasn't born in the South for nothing!) "Now if you will hold it steady, maybe I can do it." It reminded me of the Calgary Stampede, roping a dogie.

Dave moved furniture for me. This inspired him to put brackets on the coffee table that we bought in Hawaii on our honeymoon. This is to keep the top from slipping off every time I put my feet on it.

"Come feel this cigarette burn—it's still hot!"

"Dave, that has been covered by the couch the last three months. I think we might have noticed if it was still hot."

By noon I was putting more water from my forehead and armpits into that carpet than was coming from the pump in the infernal machine.

There is one major flaw in renting a contraption like this—besides the fact that they are always leakier than a two-year-old in a swimming pool (and only slightly less expensive). It is the obsession to get one's money's worth out of a twenty-four-hour stint at torture. I was determined to finish the entire house (only seven rooms are carpeted), and by the time it is finished, the renter is finished. I always use too much detergent, cannot find a bucket that doesn't have a split in the side, and without fail forget to buy de-foamer. I don't even know what it does since I've never remembered to get it.

But oh, what satisfaction it is when I empty that leaky pail into the sink! That marvelous black water! It is the dirt my kids have tracked in from my front yard. It is Cedar Key cat hair. It's a bit of road grease reminding me that Dave travels a lot. It's almost as good as reminiscing over cleaning the refrigerator.

I'll do it again and probably again. Knowing Dave, he will probably buy me a case of Steam Cleaner next week. The possibilities are endless. In case you aren't familiar with it, a movie was made a few decades ago called *Hardware Wars*. It reminded me of this afternoon's adventure.

Living and Loving the House Guests
August 1989

There is something about knowing you will have household guests that can strike terror into even the Pearl Mestas of the world. I've never claimed to be a world class house-keeper but I know my friends and they already know that. I do not run out and buy new sheets or have the house fumigated. I can't claim to have enough beds to go around but I have plenty of sleeping

bags and extra mattresses.

I like to cook ahead simply because I'd rather talk to the folks instead of watching water boil. I might miss some of the gossip.

Dave is about as informal as I am. He teaches our guests how to make the coffee pot work and the bathtub seal. He instructs them in the fine art of nabbing ants on the kitchen counter. There are a few house rules: Whomever gets the newspaper takes out last night's trash. If you spill it, you mop it up.

I warn them that unless they love cats to keep the door shut. My cats are all too sociable at 4 AM.

The second day of our visit we introduce the guests to mullet and grits. We don't care if they've never eaten fried fish for breakfast or not. They've already been introduced to my refrigerator (open door policy) and what else can happen to them?

It is important to give guests time alone to soak up Cedar Key. It is extremely difficult not to give a running narrative of the history of the salt marsh or the plight of its denizens. We've learned to seal our lips and let our friends see for themselves. I'm still not sure what being a good hostess means—but the folks keep coming and I sure like seeing them.

Will the Patron Saint of Transmissions Please Stand Up?
September 1991

Long before the Red Phone or hot-lines became household words, my mother and St. Anthony strung together two coffee cans with string and communicated regularly. It was a party-line and sometimes they would ring up St. Jude if the situation seemed "impossible." Mama rarely found it necessary to call the Chief Executive Officer in heaven to help her out with mere earthly problems. Lost car keys, insurance papers, birth certificates, a recipe for chicken turned up without fail. Eyeglasses were found as was money for next month's mortgage payment. This wasn't a demonstration of superstition, it was/is a fact. My dad, the skeptic of all skeptics, was known to say: "Lorraine, pray to St. Anthony."

For those of us of the Catholic faith, I try all the rational approaches to solutions for problems, then I pray about them.

Sally came over to my house this morning. She was going to help me get ready for a vacation. I was to drive her back to town. I hadn't counted on this turn of events but resigned myself to unsheathing the little green four-wheeled gourd. This is the car that refuses to go forward at less than 40 MPH. Today, it refused to back up at any speed. We inched toward the poles in first, second, third and fourth gears. We pushed the car back to a safe starting place in neutral. Neither of us are 90 lb weaklings but we couldn't push that car to a position where it could choose among its forward gears. I learned 25 years ago that cursing a gear box never helps. St. Anthony couldn't find reverse gear either. I know, because I asked him. It was apparent that he had more important things to do this morning than get me into town and Sally home. We are figuring that we would need to have an airlift to turn the car around: I will suggest backing it into the bay next time (the carport bay, that is).

Sally said, "You know, every time I come over here there is something like this going on..." I've tried to explain that I don't make up the stories. Nancy at the *Beacon* was ever so nice: she suggested that I walk to town. I suggested that she was sounding a little bit too much like David. I've left a message on St. Anthony's machine: "Find Reverse and Let Me Know." He suggested that I call St. Jude direct. This was truly an impossible situation.

Don't Forget To Wear Clean Underwear
September 1991

Several things happened this past week to give me pause—more than that, make me want to reform before it is too late. It started when Dave and I visited my mom at the retirement center in Dade City last Wednesday. A sweet-looking white-haired lady jumped out of her rocking chair to hold the door for me. I then looked down at the box I was carrying my mother's crochet yarn in. The little lady wanted to know where the party was. (Liquor stores do have good boxes.) We then proceeded to the elevator (which opens and closes at the end of each decade of the rosary). I politely held the photoelectric cell at bay while wondering if I could survive without my left arm. It knew I wasn't supposed to do that and gave me one of those Calvin and Hobbs leers before it retreated into its slot. We had a lively repartee with a resident who wanted to go down instead of up. At that moment, I would have had the elevator go crosswise to suit the lady but my left arm was still in shock.

The folks at Edwinola Towers are so very nice. They should, however, do something about traffic lights for the scooters in the halls and us pedestrians! I swear it reminds me of the chicken races on old Memorial Highway in Tampa when I was a teenager! (How many "points" do you get for a daughter or son-in-law?)

The second event that signaled the coming Armageddon was that sign in the sky: "This is your 10,000th used car dealer visitation in three years! You are getting no closer to the perfect vehicle!" To me, the perfect vehicle is one that allows me to sleep the entire way to a destination, synchronizes its fill-up needs with my emptying needs, doesn't develop mysterious puddles on the right rear floor and has a sound system that would rival Studio B in Nashville. It should also have four tires and an engine. (Four, six, eight of them, it doesn't matter to me!) I'd prefer it to be some shade of blue and not have klieg lights on the roof. Dave is pickier: I know I will get this wrong, but so has every car salesman: "Five on the floor, except in the years ending with 7's or 9's. No Eights, No Fours, except in '86, but that is too old. No '90's or 91's—we can't afford them. King Cab is fine if there is a topper but Susan doesn't like most of the toppers.

We knew we were persona non grata when I asked if anyone ever kicked tires anymore. (And may I please fill up my water jug at your cold water fountain?) There was a sign in the sky! "Go Home!" Timely advice! It was raining again! Crossing the Number 4 Bridge is always a thrill—to come home to Cedar Key.

I am not left without transportation when Dave makes his treks to the Big Town. It's just that I feel so conspicuous in that green Mercedes! A pickup truck, it is not!

Later in the week a third sign appeared. I, who pride myself on deciphering any word that even comes close to English, received a booklet from a Theosophism Society. My first reaction was: "Which one of my relatives is trying to reform me now?" Since I didn't know what the word meant, I looked it up. (Students, are you listening?) I reckon I came across as something of a mystic, trying to embrace essential truth underlying all systems of science, religion and philosophy. (Gee, I really didn't think I was doing that!) Sometimes it seems the most philosophical I ever get is: "Why do the bugs eat the string beans and not the black-eyed peas?" or "Why do cats choose to vomit hairballs on oriental rugs rather than tile floors?" I appreciate the thought behind the 52-cent postage and really and truly like learning about the ways people think. So often all I hear or see is that they don't think!

The week chugged on as weeks have wont to do. I knew this was a year to remember when Dave scheduled a mountain cabin for my birthday. For many years, my birthdays have been memorable: I got caught in a flash flood in Utah sleeping alone in a cave; the two of us were nearly floated into some New Mexico river another time. I spent one in a hurricane and many more just wondering what would happen next. That should give you an indication of what to expect! That Dave should actually arrange for me to have a real bed, TV, VCR, electric lights and running water (from a faucet) must mean something. I'm not sure what, yet. I'm taking the lantern and the sleeping bags and the long johns and plenty of beer. (Never can tell about those North Carolina counties.)

My latest signal to beware was that we actually had folks climb our stairs (the wrong door, of course) and I had to hunt for the right doorbell! Before me were three young ladies: one the spokesperson, another, a toddler—the foil, and another perhaps a student of door to door-ism. I gave these folks lots of credit, since it must be a labor of love to exact my presence at home at any given hour—and to find me hospitable even more.

For those of you who haven't visited my car you won't understand that I do not do bumper stickers; I do door stickers This particular door is a collate of "Save The Everything!"

She says: "I see you care about the world." (I grimaced.)

"Not exactly. I care about myself, my children, my friends."

"Do you think the world will be paradise again?" I stared! I stumbled.

She suggested that I read a tract about paradise.

If I had been a really nice person I would have invited them in. It slipped my mind. If she had come in, if I had been so good (which I wasn't), she would have known paradise. It is my home on a Saturday afternoon.

I had to look up the word Armageddon: a battle between forces of good and evil that portends the end of the world. I reckon I can wait for a few more signs in the sky and people at my door sill.

It sure is nice to live in a country where I can say these things. It's a joy to be able to talk out ones' thoughts. This is our country and you don't have to agree with me at all. Isn't that nice?

Incredible? You'd Better Believe It!
July 1991

The problem with writing this column is that lots of people think I make up the stories. When your life reads like a sit-com and soap opera, travelogue and adventure series, you don't have to write fiction. What I thought I'd do one rainy afternoon last month was write my obituary. If this sounds morbid, let me assure you that everyone should try it at least once. Perhaps I'd been watching too many of those after-death documentaries on TV, but I was fairly certain that I would not be allowed to take my laptop keyboard with me where ever I would be going and wanted to make sure there were no typos and God forbid, no misplaced apostrophes.

Saintly David came in and peered over my shoulder. He knows by now that if there is one thing about which I am absolutely paranoid is to have someone read my writing while it is being composed. I lose all manner of cool, my train of thought is immediately derailed and I go into sobbing fits of hysteria.

"Do you want lunch?" he innocently asked.

"Lunch? Can't you see I am writing my obituary?"

"Oh, is the PMS that bad?"

"You can be included in this column if you don't stop peering over my shoulder under the guise of being nice."

Most obituaries are pretty dull things. I've never really cared when a person was born or where. Suffice to assume that they were born and died. Those are givens in any culture. Also, if I am close enough to a person to even care if they died, I should care enough to know if they were sick or had an accident. Some people, however, do slip through the cracks and can evoke some pretty sensational memories when we discover, through an obituary, that they died. So, maybe there is a reason for an obituary after all.

I continued to think about the things I'd want noted in my own death notice. Most of my vital statistics are on some public computer someplace. Did you know, however, that I drove a bulldozer through the streets of Gainesville? (Sometime in 1960.) A *borrowed* bulldozer! That at one time I had memorized over two-dozen scandalous limericks? (If I could have carried a tune, I would have been dangerous!) That I once took guitar lessons? That I was expelled from the first grade? That I dyed my hair flaming red? Important stuff? You bet! Incredible? Not really.

How much more fun would it be for my friends (all three of them) to remember me this way. (I've simply removed all the things anyone would already know anyway.)

"Susan lived until she died." An incredible life. You'd better believe it!

Having written the obituary, I decided to revise my will. One might think that it is an advantage to having an in-house lawyer who specializes in this sort of thing. Wrong! While I want to divvy up each silver dollar and cup and saucer to individuals, he advises me that this a stupid, insane, worthless, inane and altogether dumb thing to do. (Now, would he talk to a paying client like that?) Do it his way or get another lawyer!

Considering the fact that there would *be* no silver dollars if I hired another attorney, I complied with his dictum. The proper way to avoid having an estate tied up is to do the will in very basic fashion and have all the trinkets listed in a letter to a trusted family member or friend who will keep up with the obituaries and come forward when your name appears. This of course required that I 1) find a friend, and 2) write another letter. The whole idea of this thing was getting out of hand.

Lunch was ready. I figured the obituary could wait. The kids would only spend the silver dollars anyway and drink Chardonnay out of the demitasse cups. So what if nobody knows about the fun on the bulldozer and can't find the twenty-four verses to "In the Clover..." Life itself is incredible. Believe it and live it!

Edibles

*The Bean Queen of Cedar Key at the
1989 Garden Club Chowder Cook-Off*

How to Stuff a Wild Manicotti
October 1988

The year was 1988. We'd moved into our brand new house on Boogie Ridge. At that time there were only a handful of us who were year-round residents. Steven had moved to Gainesville to an apartment near Santa Fe Community College. Dave was in Orlando five days a week. The two cats and I held down the fort. I've never been at a loss to find ways to entertain myself. It was about then that I decided to learn to cook Italian—something other than my standby spaghetti or my "Come to Dinner" Lasagna. By the time I'd finished stuffing that new manicotti I had a new "career." Nobody knew it then but that's when I started taking writing—not cooking (ha ha)—seriously.

A manicotti is by its nature a very docile piece of tubular pasta measuring about six inches long and one inch across. (I measured this with a yardstick so I can be sure.) It stays fairly quiet throughout the boiling process. The recipe is straightforward as to the creation of a cheesy stuffing. No matter that it requires at least fourteen different types of cheeses, none of which I had on hand or frozen from last year's Christmas baskets.

Out came the trusty food processor which grates, slices, chews and masticates food—all with the flip of a switch and assembly of its handles, cams, lids and gears. But first, to the market to secure the necessary cheeses! Once the stuffing was completed and the pasta boiled, rinsed, drained and appropriately "set aside," I found that I had more stuffing than manicotti.

Back to the market for more manicottis. These were duly boiled, rinsed, drained and set aside. The stock in The Market at Cedar Key rose three points that afternoon and owner Harry Hooper was undoubtedly urging his staff to encourage my culinary efforts. The recipe blandly states: "Spoon the stuffing into the manicotti..." I should add "first grab the sucker firmly before it wiggles up your sleeve and down your pants leg to the floor." If you don't, you will wind up with cheese stuffing in your shirt pocket. This is very much akin to pouring spaghetti sauce down a length of garden hose.

I took a hint from the Galloping Gourmet of yore and realized that this was definitely a three-sherry dish. Two for the dish and one for the cook.

Everything was progressing nicely after the first several tries. That is until their invisible little zippers began opening down the sides. What resulted was an open-face ecru-colored lasagna. I relegated this first platter to the file in the refrigerator that says, "Eat after midnight by candlelight."

Two boxes of pasta later I had six perfectly formed, stuffed manicotti, three platters of the "Eat after midnight by candlelight," and a kitchen that was glued together by mozzarellas and ricottas. My food processor has been in soak for 24 hours, and I have a new and interesting grout on my countertops. Very Italian.

Today I will make Chicken Cacciatore. At least I am sure that the chicken is dead. I wasn't so sure about those manicottis!

Some Cooking Memories

Just the other day Steve (that's my Number Three Son) and I were sitting on a log in the woods discussing the merits of our trail lunch that I had lovingly prepared that morning.

"So what's wrong with bagels and peanut butter? Here you have the basic four food groups: bread, protein, an apple for fruit, and some high-fat beef jerky. All we need is a green vegetable."

He must have been thinking about the refrigerator at home when he asked: "Mom, is mold a green vegetable?"

"I don't think so. I'm growing our own supply of penicillin!".

The evening before, I whomped up trail chicken and yellow rice. We carried a full dehydrated chicken in a baggie. For your information a chicken weighs approximately 1.5 ounces, rice 6 ounces., and green beans dehydrated, 2 ounces. Let me tell you that chicken fluffed up to taste like the real thing sans feathers and bones.

The breakfast didn't fair so well. I was frying some biscuits on a one-burner backpacking stove. In the process of cooking and not burning, they absorbed one-half pound of margarine (our weekly supply of cholesterol).

This reminds me of another trip in the Boundary Waters Canoe Area, an Outward Bound canoeing trip in Minnesota. A gentleman from our group was making pizza. This man was a professor from (wow) FSU and had never had his fingers in any kind of dough (of any kind) before. He was the dignified sort: neatly cropped beard and mustaches (at least for the first two days). He was the one who seriously asked where to plug in his hair dryer. It was his turn to cook while the rest of us splashed in the cold water. I tired of icy water in a hurry hurry and returned to where professor Jay was kneading dough and needing help. Instead of embers he had a roaring fire that kept fogging his glasses and enough smoke to cure a hog. Eventually the fire burned down to the hot rock stage and, between the two of us, we shaped something that looked like a pizza. We piled on ingredients: tomato, pinon nuts, sausage and probably a chipmunk or two. At that moment of triumph, we felt we should share this with the world. You are the first, however, to hear about Hot Rock Pizza.

Another great triumph of culinary expertise was on yet another Outward Bound trip, hiking in the North Carolina hills. Our group was searching for the water hole and down to about a pint of water each. I was badly in need of a sugar jolt and was getting increasingly cranky. The young man's name was Eric and I told him that I was going to make us a milkshake with my remaining water. I poured in the powdered milk, some brown sugar, and some honey and shook the bottle violently. The water was only moderately cool. It tasted divine. Once we found a new supply of water, the entire group made this concoction and extolled it's virtues. Another "splash hit!" A few months later Eric wrote me from his college. He said he had made this milkshake for his roommate and himself and that it had lost something in the translation. He said it was horrible! Hunger does wonderful things to the taste buds, doncha' think?

When I was about seven, I won a prize for my Green Tea Cake. (My dad was into green tea at the time.) I was balanced on a kitchen cabinet drawer to make me tall enough to reach the counter and operate the mixer. Inadvertently, I knocked a full box of green tea into the cake mix. My mother would not let me throw the batter away and jokingly said: "Enter it in the contest." I did, and the rest is history. I won coupons for about fifty Betty Crocker cake mixes.

Then there was a promotion campaign for "Vadall." What

this stuff really was, I will never know. It cost too much for my family to buy but apparently was some sort of dairy cream cheese product. It was heavily advertised in the early '50s in Tampa. That particular summer we were eating a lot of fresh peaches. I would smoosh the peaches up with sugar and milk and eat or drink this stuff. My entry was to add 1 teaspoon full of Vadall to the blend. This entry earned me cash money and my name announced on TV. Vadall went off the market soon after.

Nowadays, Dave and I have running battles over recipes. He uses them time after time as if they are carved in stone. I read them and "adjust" (which means I usually can't find them again). For example, I've been making eggplant Parmesan for as long as I have been eating eggplant. My family loves this dish almost as much as they love lasagna. David, however, had to get a recipe book to make it "the right way." I didn't quarrel with the fact that he sliced the eggplant lengthwise or dredged it in seasoned flour before frying it. It's just that I make mine with rings and no flour and season each batch as I go. I happen to like eggplant skins; his recipe said to peel the fruit. His recipe of course is the "right way." Mine is Mine.

Kids' Kooking Korner
February 1990

Look who's talking! The mother of the Whiz that created a year's worth of peanut butter frosting while attempting to make Christmas cookies; mother of the Microwave King; and inventor of the World's only "guaranteed to cure anything" hot sauce. Trust me, any kid that is hungry enough will learn to cook. Traditionally, it has fallen to the female of the species to be on the business end of a fry pan or at the helm of the oven. Not so in my house. My boys called it "survival instinct." I stood by with the fire extinguisher, and instead of after dinner mints passed out Alka-Seltzer tablets.

We had some good times along the way. Even some educational times. Learning doesn't have to be boring. I've only met a handful of children who actually liked learning fractions from a school book. I have my suspicions that they were genetically warped or were born under the sign of Prime Rate. What better way to learn fractions than scooping up 1/3 cup of this and 1/3 cup of that? Measuring cups are also dandy teachers when it comes to converting the metric system to avoirdupois or vice-versa. "What's a milliliter, Mom?"

Not everyone agrees with my theories on kitchen creativity. One of the most outspoken critics is Father David. He contends that if it wasn't written by Fannie Farmer or Julia Child or by somebody on the staff of Florida Sportsman, it is just another concoction. David is the type of person who polishes measuring spoons and counts grains of salt when he cooks. Not to criticize his school of thought, but it is a whole lot more fun my way.

The first—and most important thing—when you set out to cook is to figure out what you want to eat. It's a good idea the first time out on the range to have some sort of recipe. Locate the ingredients either from the pantry or go to the store and buy them. (After the first time, you can get creative and start the eternal substitution.) Put these out, in order, on the kitchen counter top. Put on an apron, have plenty of paper towels handy. Put all the equipment out on the counter too. It's gruesome to have to look for a sifter or a mixer when your hands are full of gooey stuff.

Now, let's cook!

It's pretty sneaky to have to resort to teaching our children to read and do math by the way of their stomachs but it does work. By the time they realize they are reading package ingredients they will already have had a nutrition lesson, a chemistry seminar and a hygiene course. Chances are you will have made an Act of Contrition and thus affirmed your place in the Kitchen of the Hereafter. It was my brother's job to prepare dinner at least once a week when my mom's shop stayed open until 9 PM. Jack was twelve and I was five and usually I went home with him as his aide-de-camp. This night we were making pot-roast in the new pressure cooker. (We did *not* have to scour the ceiling the next day!) That was probably the best pot-roast I've ever eaten! Jack made me peel the carrots and potatoes while all he did was watch the thingamajig clatter on top of the pot. I knew it wasn't fair. He looked at me with that smug big-brother look and said: "Hey, I figured out how to work this thing, didn't I?" My five-year-old mind agreed: he could read directions. He could do numbers. He could cook!

Children Should Understand the "Mother Syndrome"
December 1989

My children are only half perfect. After all, they did have two parents! The part that is perfect is 100%. They get their sense of the absurd from me. They inherited their biceps from their father (thank God!) The way that a mother treats a grown son is, in my estimation, uniformly insane and I am no exception to the rule. Prospective daughters-in-law should understand the rules of the road before they travel in this direction.

My sons have all liked to eat and in order to eat they had to learn how to cook. They aren't picky eaters and if it is dead or not nailed down they will probably at least take a bite. They also like to invent dishes. They don't always read directions. Steven once created a year's worth of peanut-butter frosting while attempting to make cookies. (He'd used Cremora instead of flour.) It came then as no surprise when he presented me with a jar of his Hot-and-Spicy Tomato Meat Sauce when I visited him in Gainesville this week.

He had gone so far as to put the ingredients on the old Ragu bottle. I asked him why he didn't compute the calorie count as well. Steven had grown the tomatoes on his patio, crumbled two hamburger patties, and added at least ten of my own Cedar Key cayennes—which accounted for the hot and spicy label.

I suggested that he just make some spaghetti and we would eat it there (hospitals are closer). The pasta was a perfect *al dente*. Steve said it was raw. The sauce was palatable. Steven said, "Mom, why is it so watery?"

"I'm thinking that maybe it is the liter of tomato juice that you used." Don't get me wrong—I was thoroughly appreciative of the delightful dinner (that I didn't have to cook).

Sons are marvelous creatures. They will surprise you at every turn. When I am a guest in Steven's house I am reminded to turn off the bathroom light, flush the toilet and hang up the towel. I did something right someplace along the line.

Steven offers you his recipe for Hot and Spicy:

Frozen hamburger patties, crumbled (in this case with an ice pick); 6 tomatoes, squashed; 5-6 cayenne peppers, humiliated; 1 large can tomato juice.

Dump all of this into a pot and cook for awhile. Put it over some half-done spaghetti or linguine or what ever is in the cupboard. If you have any Parmesan cheese in the refrigerator you can put that on top. I like this with a salad, but unless I go to the store I've already used my tomatoes for the sauce. Mom uses mayonnaise on her salads and I hate mayonnaise but you can use it if you like.

If any of you out there in reader-world have children who even resemble this one, I'd like to hear from you. Their brilliance lights up my life.

Blame It on the Italians!
January 1989

My husband likes Italian food. In fact, David likes food, period. When we married, he was already an accomplished spaghetti chef but wanted me to go and reach for the heights and depths and breads (sic) my soul could accomplish.

He suggested that I take a course in Italian cooking. Now I ask you, did you ever try to find something in the "Yellow Pages" that said "Italian cooking classes?"

It did sound like a wonderful diversion from spooning Gerber's onto Ritz crackers for Jimmy to gum around and spit on the floor three times a day. (My son was quite the baby gourmand.)

I found a class—in Rome (Italy). Since the airfare alone would have paid for a year of dining out, he instead bought me a cookbook at a garage sale. *The Romagnioff's Table* I think it was. I learned to make lasagna from the back of the Mueller's noodle box in the meantime.

David had, however, planted a wicked weed seed in my mind to take cooking classes. I'd opted for sewing in Home Economics and except for wonderful potato salad and angel food cakes, I wasn't too proficient in the culinary arts.

One day he arrived home and I announced "Do you like Chinese food?" The closest we'd come to authentic Chinese was putting together a La Choy canned dinner and adding canned boned chicken. "After all," I reasoned, "they did invent spaghetti." Thus began my three-year stint at Lily Tang's cooking school.

There were about eight of us gathered around Lily's large round table for our first lesson. She sliced, diced, minced, soaked, steamed and we watched. Then we ate. These were the days when one did not immediately become a *persona non grata* by pulling out a package of cigarettes. The Winston people sat together and the Kool people took the other side of the table. The non-smokers retired to the bathroom for a burst of fresh air.

Along with the food, which was exotic enough, was the history and philosophy that came along with class–buy quantities of ginger root, bean sprouts, cornstarch, sherry, black mushrooms and whatever vegetable was featured that day. The real test came a few months into our third year. My sorority was sponsoring a series of *international* luncheons to raise money for something or other.

I said, "Joan, help me cook for forty women."

She answered, "You've got to be out of your mind."

"Of course, I know that, but will you help me?"

"Sure, why not?"

To appreciate the appeal of such a luncheon you must understand that it is in the finest of oriental traditions to have one course per guest: that meant forty dishes. First off, Joan didn't like the slant of my broccoli. I swear she used a protractor to cut hers.

The kids would come home from school and find strips of black mushroom marinating and not one ounce of peanut butter in sight. They got the rejected sesame cookies and almond tofu.

"Mom's into Chinese cooking," Davy III explained apologetically to a soccer buddy who was wolfing down a plate of Mandarin orange slices that were supposed to be the dessert of the century.

The day finally arrived that we transported all of our half-baked food to the hostess' home for final preparation. Allison had a refrigerator the size of a bank vault and industrial strength stoves and ovens. My whole, but de-boned, duck (you figure that one out) was duly stuffed with pearl rice; we had four soups: hot/sour; won ton; egg flower and napa. There was oyster sauce beef; beef and broccoli; tomato beef; wontons fried to a crisp golden brown; clams on the shell; spring rolls; fried rice; Chinese roast pork; and I think a million desserts.

I've forgotten more than I ate that day. We served six different types of teas in different style pots, had a Hunan steamed dish with pearl meatballs.

When all were served, Joan said: "Why did I let you talk me into this?" I said "Blame the Italians." About that time we said almost in chorus: "Know what we forgot? *Plain Rice!*" (Who cared?)

In Quest of the Holy Grille
March 1989

There comes a time in the life of every home appliance that one must consider quietly letting it go, arranging for a space for it in the Bronson Happy Hill Landfill.

You can usually begin with a pre-need plan about a week before the warranty runs out. Not so with our trusty, rusty gas grille. That item had so many transplants it hardly resembled the original and kept on firing year after year, chicken after chicken, rib after rib. It had, however, become dangerous. It had this funny little tendency to fall over with or without flames attached. Dave had gotten to the point he would allow no one near it during the cooking process except himself and the fire extinguisher.

There came the day that I announced that we were going to have an Oyster Party: a "shuck 'em and eat 'em sort of thing" (and of course, put a few on the grill for those who just can't handle the real thing raw—like son David).

Husband looked at me with one of those looks and said: "Well, I guess I'll have to fix the grill. Again!" The rest of the morning was spent with him looking for something to transplant the last transplant with. Certainly they still make replacement parts for this obviously classic design.

"When did you say this party was?"

"Tomorrow!"

"Oh! Why did you say we needed roast oysters?"

"Your son won't eat raw oysters and that is my entire—got it?—*entire* menu!" I got another of those now-I-know-you're-crazy looks and Dave suggested sending David III out for a bowl of soup when he got here.

The next morning we set out in search of a new gas grill. Armed with last year's consumer's guide, the next hour I spent reading him model numbers of *best buys* from what appeared to be obscure grill manufacturers in the Ukraine. We boned up on features to look for, features to avoid, hazards and *vast improvements*.

None of this made much difference since the prices had jumped thirty times since we bought the one that was being retired. I got another one of those looks. "Tell me again why we need to buy a grill today!" I smiled innocently and for once kept my mouth shut.

Dave is not one to be rushed into buying something. As most women who have been married longer than 24 hours realize, men must necessarily be convinced that any purchase be essential to the health and welfare of the family—be this a fishing reel or a vacuum cleaner—or a gas grill.

His argument with himself ran something like this: "Summer is coming up and we will use it a lot. I don't like the house to be hot—the air conditioning bills will be less." Well, so far, so good, Susan!

It was then that I made the mistake of telling him that these things came unassembled. He did concede to look at them. I'm sure his visions were those of Christmas Eve's past—assembling swing-sets by moonlight and tricycles in the living room by candle flame.

We picked up two of the three children in Gainesville and set out on the Quest for the Holy Grille. I suggested that we opt for a simple charcoal dish type thing. (My strategy is a fine honed piece of machinery.) "Not economical in the long run," intones the master who has by now assumed control.

"Just tell me one more time why we need this thing today."

Jimmy comes to the rescue. "Dad, just *buy* it—I'll put it together." (This was getting out of hand.) "Besides, I'm hungry."

The story continues back in Cedar Key where Jimmy has five thousand (or what looked like it) nuts and bolts and washers lined up neatly on a log. (I cannot watch anymore.) Jimmy is confident and competent. He requires some liquid soap and water to do a leak test on the tank. Oh dear, am I really letting this child play with a flammable gas?

The guests came a bit later. Jim was still in his work clothes doing the things college juniors find most satisfying—driving their mothers crazy. He held out a hand to one, and with a shy apology said: "You see, Mom wanted this grill and I'm building it." He shot me one of those genetically inherited looks that said: "Tell me one more time why you wanted this thing today?"

On Cannery Row
June 1990

Twenty-five years after writing this column I have filled over one-thousand Ball jars without losing a consumer. Of course, as they say, past performance is no guarantee of future results.

Television garden shows can be dangerous to your health. Those fellows who go out into their "North Forty's" and pluck tomatoes and mulch the zucchini can find more ways to get me into hot water (literally) than Don Johnson on *Miami Vice*.

Came the day that our postage stamp garden was producing in abundance (after the birds finished and before the caterpillars and before the second team of birds moved in). It was sometime before the raccoon went ten rounds with the Rottweiler in the deck garden and in his frenzy took the cukes and part of the railing with him on the way down. I had the freezer full of zucchini and bok choy and was anticipating the later tomatoes and beans and okra. "Wherever are we going to put this stuff?"

Dave got that look in his eye. I wasn't sure whether to find my wooden stake or my silver bullet.

"Why don't we 'can' it?"

"Do you know how to can?"

"No, but I've got a garden show tape that tells you."

Now I knew I was in trouble.

On this show, a kindly and countrified gentleman stands in the middle of a gleaming stainless steel kitchen. He can locate a large pot from the cupboard without calling in a team of archaeologists. His wooden spoon has never been used to plant lilies (I can tell). He has jars and lids that fit each other. He has an apron that has never been used as a Halloween cape. He doesn't have band-aids on three of his ten fingers. His produce is pre-plucked, pre-washed and patted dry. There are no mysterious stains on his dishcloths used for draining. He makes it look like any idiot could do this. Well, I'm not just *any* idiot!

Thoughts of little gremlins like Clostridium Botulinum hung in the back of my mind. "Dave, I really feel better with a pressure canner." At least that postponed the inevitable: we didn't own a pressure canner—yet. Two weeks later we owned a pressure cooker/canner. It displaced the rice cooker on the top of the refrigerator, which displaced the wok, which went on top of the microwave, which displaced the hot pot holders. At least we wouldn't have to go on a "dig" to find it since it is as big as an old fashioned refrigerator monitor (compressor) that used to sit on top of early fridges.

Time came to try our hand(s) at canning. One son thoughtfully mused: "Where are you going to get the cans?" The boys are city bred and to them a "can" means Campbell's Soup or catfood. I conceded that it should probably be called "jarring."

What would be our first project? This required researching cookbooks, canning books, preserving books and scraps of paper with ancient recipes that may have been written in Sanskrit. The problem with Dave and me doing anything like this is that we find ourselves reading the entire book and perhaps forgetting why we find ourselves reading the entire book and perhaps forgetting why we opened it in the first place. Eventually we settled on doing some relishes. He loves chow-chow and piccalilli. Unfortunately the picture that accompanied these recipes bore no resemblance to what he called chow-chow or piccalilli. We settled on "Grandma's Tomato Relish" and "Onion-Pepper Relish." Then we checked my spice cabinet. I'd always thought I could have paid my way to the Northwest Passage with the number of cans of spices in that pantry. I needed turmeric and celery seed. More than that, we hated to decimate our tomato garden; we didn't have enough green and red peppers; nor did we have ten pounds of onions, ten pounds of sugar, several gallons of various flavors of vinegar. So we went shopping. We needed a different funnel, some tongs, and lots more canning jars. I won that round and we got the pretty ones rather than the more traditional utility variety.

I said innocently: "We might want to give a jar to our friends."

"Are you kidding? I don't want any of them getting sick." (Ah, Confidence!)

We unearthed the food processor and began chopping onions and peppers. I prepared and Dave chopped. The blade started making this terrible noise and we realized that the onion was too much for the blade. Perhaps the cayenne we threw in for good measure melted it. "No problem. I can epoxy it." He did and we continued on with a slicing blade. Six times through the machine and it was as good as chopped.

The mixture cooked. I noticed the leaves on the oak trees outside shriveling. My skin was feeling sunburned. I'm not sure this mixture isn't what the Egyptians used on King Tut. It did, at least, smell divine. We began on the tomato relish while the onion pepper was being processed. This was to cook for several hours and turn a bright red. It cooked for several hours and looked like a rich barbecue sauce—by no stretch of the imagination could it be called "red." It was put in jars and processed (very pretty indeed). I proudly put labels on our handiwork.

Today, before we retire our cooker and funnel and sieve and measuring paraphernalia, I've promised Dave some chow chow and piccalilli—the kind he remembers. We did have to go to the store and buy just a few more ingredients.

One of these days we'll figure out how much each of these half-pint jars of relish cost us. I'm hoping that "you gets what you pays for."

Oysters—You Just Can't Stop
January 1989

Our first Thanksgiving in Cedar Key was a festive family affair in our picket-fence rental. Honest-to-goodness Cedar Key oysters seemed a perfect preface to the turkey and trimmings. A local oysterman was "tonging" in the close-by channel so I sent sons Steven and Jim wading to gather some. Those were the bestest, fattest, most delicious oysters in memory. Dave only half jokingly credits their quality on the number of septic tanks in the vicinity.

It was on that "other" coast of Florida that I had my first serious encounter with an oyster. I'd toyed with them on seafood platters when they were fried beyond recognition.

I just couldn't bring myself to eat the fishy tasting milk my father called "oyster stew" and even in my wildest imagination couldn't see myself swallowing one of those things raw, even if bathed in a tomatoey sauce! I had, however, mastered the art of eating raw clams several years earlier and the making of a mind-bending clam chowder. I'd clammed in Alaska, the Pacific Coast, the Chesapeake, and now was happily digging the Florida Quahogs. Dave was into New Smyrna Beach oysters.

I considered this a real no-talent operation, much like crabbing: either they were there or they weren't. (Apologies all around to you commercial folks!)

Since I love slopping in ice-cold water in January, I agreed to help Dave snare some oysters after I'd bagged enough clams for dinner. Dave measures things like oysters; if there was a three-inch requirement, he brought out his calipers.

We hammered away about two dozen of the critters—enough for a snack for him. It was going to be a real "shore dinner" what with the kids' crabbing success. We scrubbed and steamed the crab in mystic potions of spices and herbs. I chowdered the clam. The oysters, however, were to remain inviolate, eaten raw on the shell over the kitchen sink.

Disgusting! Especially so when Dave stabbed his hand to the bone with an oyster knife! As a nurse, I was pretty sure he would live, despite the self-inflicted wound and evidence all over the oysters and kitchen cabinet. I wrapped his hand, and inspected the damage, butterflied the laceration and retired him to the living room couch. If you know David at all you will understand that we almost didn't get married due to the required blood test.

Now, what was I going to do with all of those cussed oysters? He wanted them raw, by golly, he was going to get them! I picked up the yukky glove and started shucking. Not expertly, not even carefully, but shucking nonetheless. I'll admit we got quite a bit of calcium carbonate in that batch.

This is not the end of the story. The end is where David teaches me to eat them—and I do and haven't stopped since.

To Catch a Crab
September 1989

The blue crab, another of the Florida seashore "gatherables," is not for one of genteel table manners. Messy to the extreme, even revolting to some, a meal of these beauties is best shared with happily talkative friends and many pitchers of cold beer.

There are all kinds of ways to catch crabs, and some of them are best not mentioned in polite company. There are also a lot of different types of crabs and a lot of ways to serve the edible varieties.

The first time I was confronted with a platter of steamed and spiced Florida blue crab I was at a loss where to begin. We were sitting at a long wooden picnic type table that had been covered with newspaper. It wasn't a fancy place. A guy sat in the corner strumming a guitar. He had disengaged himself from his shoes an hour earlier and was pulling on a long neck between tunes. The ambiance of the place was palpable. Sunburned little kids slurped and burped. No one was rowdy because they were too busy eating crab and oyster. It takes a lot of concentration!

This place (over on the other coast) did not provide bibs or tuckers or cracking implements. I watched carefully to see what other people were doing. What ever they were doing, it was a pretty sloppy process but when the meat got to the mouth they smiled all over! I rolled up my sleeves and took instructions on what parts to eat and what parts to discard.

Blue crab legs are small in comparison to other crab legs but the meat is delicate and sweet. That is where I started. Also, it is the easiest to get at. Extricate a leg from the body and crack it—nutcrackers work well but the handle of a knife does the job: Pick, pick, pick. Then if there is anything else left, put it in your mouth. Don't waste a bit! The other appendages hold salty tidbits that must be sucked out like a soda straw. The body is a little trickier since most of us don't want to consume the contents of the crab's last dinner. The easiest way, if you don't have access to a sink, to clean out the contents is with a paper napkin. Just scoop it out. The crabmeat of the body is even more delicate and tender than the legs. Lungs will not hurt you—the ruffled white mass in the body; I don't eat them. They are, however, surrounded by lovely white crabmeat. Eating a platter of blue crab is a night's work!

It was that night that I decided we needed a few crab traps. These were available at the hardware store. The crabs were willing to eat chicken necks. I was unwilling to get the crab out of the traps after the first one drew blood (mean little critters, the crabs). We learned that if we kept them in a cooler with ice, they would stay alive (never eat a dead crab!) but weren't nearly as feisty. We learned the rules for "keepies": five inches from carapace—pointy part of the body—to carapace. We don't keep females with egg sacs—an orange appendage on the underside—and we learned how to tell which are males and which are females (in some states taking of females is outlawed). I want to go crabbing again next year!

It wasn't until the mid-forties that blue crabs in Florida waters were considered more than a nuisance to Gulf fishermen. According to a source in Steinhatchee, even the more revered stone crab was a little known foodstuff. Now we know! Yum Yum!

We'll put out those traps that Dave just bought at a Cedar Key yard sale. I'll cook the catch the simple way: steamed with a little seafood seasoning and let the guests do the work.

> **Make Plans NOW!**
> **The Cedar Key Garden Club First Annual Chowder Cook Off!**
> If You Think Your Chowder Is The Best, Then Why Not Put It To The Test!
> November 30, 1991
> 11:00 am til...?
> Cedar Key City Park
> For information call 543-5435

Cedar Key Simmers Up Some Chowder
November 1991

CEDAR KEY–A garden club, an Indian burial mound and mass quantities of chowder from secret recipes will all have something in common today in Cedar Key.

The Cedar Key Garden Club is working to preserve an Indian burial mound on Sixth Street through a fund-raising chowder cook-off.

"If you think your chowder is the best, then why not put it to the test" is the slogan for the first annual cook-off, which is open to individuals as well as restaurants.

Entrants are being asked to provide at least three gallons of their favorite chowder, soup or bisque, but to preserve long-held family secrets, no recipe is required.

A panel of food critics from across the state will be judging the entries and promise to award first-, second- and third-place prizes sometime in the afternoon, or when the kettles are empty, whichever comes first. To ensure that the judging is impartial, each entry will be tagged with a number, rather than a name.

Spectators are asked to bring along $5 and an appetite at 11 AM or after. Following the judges' samplings, the entries will be served on an "all you can eat for $5" basis at the city park.

The Gainesville Sun

The Taste of Success—First Annual Cedar Key Chowder Cook-Off a Hit!
November 1991

With pots bubbling, the crowds came in to sample. Touted with a saying, "If you think your chowder is the best, then put it to the test," proved to be a challenge many couldn't resist.

In an attempt to raise much needed funds for the restoration of the Indian Burial Mound at the Cedar Key Lions Community Center, President Annette Haven blazed against negative attitudes, confident that this would prove to be an enjoyable event. And enjoyable it was. Over 300 people purchased tickets to sample the concoctions claimed to be the favored best.

Entered in the contest were Susan Roquemore with her Bean Soup; Annette Haven with her Fish Chowder; Cedar Cove Inn with Corn & Crab Chowder; L.C. Smith and his Fish and Shrimp Chowder; Mary Jo Cresswell representing the Garden Club entered Fish Chowder; The Fabulous Island Room entered their Oyster Rockefeller Bisque.

The West Hernando Chamber of Commerce Restaurant Association sent up their representative, Chef Manfred Schwalenberg with his Mystic Island Clam Chowder; Tina Hooper entered her Corn and Cheese Chowder; and Manualla Clark came all the way from St. Petersburg to enter her Portuguese Clam Chowder, which was noted as a cholesterol-free chowder.

Put to the ultimate test were judges Cindy Bertlesen, who writes a weekly column in the *Beacon* called "Thoughts Of Food and Such," and John Paul Jones, Jr., editor of *Florida Living* magazine. Mr. Jones also has on his resume such achievements as being a newspaper reporter and editor for several newspapers and United Press International, as well as a journalism professor at the University of Florida, where he later became the Dean of the University of Florida College of Journalism. He has been active and fundamental in the Florida Press Association for many years, and was inducted into the Florida Newspaper Hall Of Fame in 1989. He, and his wife, Marion, have traveled throughout the area tasting, from Wild Beasts in Georgia, to the St. Augustine Chowder Challenge.

The judging was all handled by numbered cups, and the winners names were not disclosed until the beginning of the entertainment at noon.

The first place trophy, along with the $100 prize was taken by Chef Manfred Schwalenberg's Mystic Island Clam Chowder. Second place was taken by the chowder made by Mary Jo Creswell representing the Cedar Key Garden Club, who won $50 and a plaque. Third place was taken by Susan Roquemore's butter bean and ham hock soup, which came with whole cayenne peppers floating about, and earned her a plaque, $25 and the nickname "Bean Queen."

Chef Manfred Schwalenberg's Mystic Island Clam Chowder

4 quarts clam stock
1 teaspoon fresh garlic
1 pound diced onions
2 pounds diced celery
2 pounds diced carrots
2 pounds diced potatoes
1 pound green pepper
1 pound red pepper
1 pound fresh leek
1 quart chopped tomatoes
Sachet Bag
2 tablespoons salt
1/2 teaspoon fresh ground pepper
1 tablespoon Worchestershire

Mix all ingredients together. Fifteen minutes before serving, add three pints of chopped clams and four tablespoons of fresh chopped parsley. Top soup in cup with oyster crackers.

Diary of a Bean Queen
December 1991

"It was a dark and stormy night..." I'd been summoned by my trusty leader to round up the crock pots. While some people collect diamonds and emeralds, I have a cache of crocks. David makes his pickles in some of them; I house his breeding pepper stock in others. Some, however, are reserved for beans! Let it be known that the humble bean has made it into the winner's circle! The fact of the matter is, I like beans.

The event was the very first Cedar Key Chowder Cook-off—sponsored by the Cedar Key Garden Club, which as everyone knows is very dear to my heart. I'd entered something (mostly David's money) to enter the thingie and had messed up every pot in the house in the process (don't get too imaginative here). By Wednesday I had a freezer full of rejected macaroni and cheese soup (something I dearly love if made correctly, which mine wasn't); garbanzo beans that I crave; and black beans (Tampa style) that were a disaster. Everyone knows that my chili could make a Texan take his boots off and the clam chowder (for which I could find no clams) is equally effective. By Wednesday, I was looking at butter beans. These are the big fat kind cooked in enough ham to call this island Cholesterol City.

On Thanksgiving Day, which happens any day of the week in my house, two of our three off-spring sprung home. The eldest is an inveterate bean soup hater.

"Mom! You *aren't* making bean soup, are you?"

How many ways can he hate bean soup? Let us count the ways! I smiled benignly and said: "Your father *likes* my bean soup!" (That explains a lot of things.)

The crock pots were lined along the counter top and bubbling merrily to themselves each with his or her own ham hock. I woke Saturday morning knowing that either something was terribly wrong in the kitchen or someone had sabotaged the Cook-off. The smell was wonderful but frightening. Knowing full well that Davy hates beans, I could not accuse him of destroying anything edible. "Someone," however, had left one of the pots on "high" and had created bean-paste. (This pot with its contents was donated to the Landfill.)

Meanwhile, back at the park: Tables were set up. Sons were burdened into service. Ladies brought their sweets and gentlemen toted their cool drinks. Others ladled.

I was tooling around the park with my plastic bag, looking all the world like the bag lady I am, when I overheard a nice comment (my friend Dotti used to tell me I had ears like a bat). "That's the way this place is. They even pick up the cans."

This "Bean Queen" wants to thank you all for making Cedar Key what she is and what she can be.

During the day, we heard more and more comments: "Please keep Cedar Key the way it is." We're going to have to try and work at it, but there is a treasure here worth preserving. We want to "Put the Cedar Back in Cedar Key!" A goal of the Garden Club. Plant a Cedar Tree! For that matter, plant a bean!

Weather Or Not

The Great Christmas Freeze of 1989

Snowflake of Cedar Key
January 1990

The only snowflakes I saw this week were in a hairbrush, but the weatherman correctly predicted other Arctic characteristics reliably. What he didn't predict was that I would be walking around my house looking like a World War I snow trooper. I've been cold before (in Alaska in the rain, for example) and fooling around the Alpine Grossglockner in a gale force wind and once in a leaky tent in Minnesota's Boundary Waters. Never did I expect my fingers to turn blue and threaten to break off on the keyboard while writing from my "cozy nest" in Cedar Key.

The heating system in our house is like the family: generally obtuse! It is a fine modern system that only works with a temperature above forty degrees. Now, I am not Eskimo but I can live with temperatures around forty by layering my parkas. We also have a cute little wood-burning stove and a supply of seasoned oak and cedar kindling. It works fine for romantic evenings when the wind isn't blowing and it isn't raining freezing water outside from the northeast. On those occasions (did you notice that the northeast winds are the coldest?) our living room begins to take on the feeling and flavor and smell of the inside of a mullet smoke house. One cannot open the windows because of the wind and rain. I begin to search for the vintage gas mask since oak smoke is the one thing that I confess allergy. The modern smoke alarms signal to the world that we have a fire going in the stove.

It is clear that David and I are unfamiliar with the vagaries of cold weather. In fact, we are downright ignorant. We first attempted to thaw out the frozen heat pump with warm water. It looked pretty funny to see him hang out the second story window poring coke glasses of warm water on the compressor which would hum nicely for about thirty seconds before kicking the breaker again. This obviously was not going to work. I pulled out the trusty hair dryer and as David blew hot air on it, the cold air blew in. This sounded like a good idea except for the fact that the house was getting colder and David got a cramp in his leg from holding the hair dryer out the window and his face was turning blue from the icy rain. We gave up and called my brother-in-law who is an air conditioning and heating man. He gave David the benefit of his expertise: "Your heat pump won't work at temperatures under forty." (Thank you, Tony!) "Try turning on your air conditioning!" We might have been the only people in Cedar Key to run the air conditioning on the coldest day of the year. The temperature outside was 26, inside 26 below!

We hadn't taken into account the reaction of the cats to cold weather. They are both used to coming and going in and out pretty much at will. Shadow is regimented in his habits and promptly at 7 AM he wanted out. When, a few hours later, he made his routine leap from the deck railing to the deck, he slid across the icy surface and smacked into the siding of the house. He glared his cross-eyed glare at Dave, regained his composure and dignity, ate his bowl of cat-wheaties, and settled in for the duration on the couch under a blanket. Miss Petunia, who is every ounce a born-and-bred Cedar Key cat, should have better survival instincts. She has, however, succumbed to the creature comforts and took longer making up her mind to go out. Once out, she took her time deciding to come in. I was a little concerned. Finally there was a banging at the door, her calico now frosted. She didn't even stop to glare but darted to Shadow!

Dave has suggested that we go fishing this afternoon. I have suggested skating on the deck instead. Do you realize that the turkey that we bought has not even been refrigerated and is still frozen solid? That when I wash dishes to get the heat from the dishwasher and that when I think of warming some bricks and laying them in the living room, this is what I call "serious cold?"

Maybe, just maybe, we could go out and rent a motel room with an old-fashioned space heater! Or go camping in the north woods! Now, if it snowed, it might have been worth it!

With Apologies to The Weatherman From Susan: Just one hour after writing this column the shouts came from the kids, "It's snowing!" Sure enough, there was enough white powder for ten thousand hairbrushes. Another hour passed and the northeast wind died and I shed a layer of parka. I guess White Christmases aren't all bad, after all.

Whither the Weathermen?
October 1989

Back in the '60's there was a radical political group called "The Weathermen." I wondered about their choice of name at the time, but since then (and having experienced another 25 years) I can understand a little better.

Weathermen (or meteorologists as they like to be called—do they really study meteors?) are by nature a radical group. If they predict rain to make the gardeners happy, the beach goers are mad. Especially so when it fails to rain. In that case both groups are after his/her head. If sun is predicted and the gardener dutifully turns on the sprinkler early in the morning and the beach goer packs the picnic and it rains, the poor weather person takes it in the neck.

What happens when the forecast is correct? Is anybody happy then? Not really!

Does anyone really like it when a hurricane is forecast and it comes down where he said it would? Or if he predicts months of drought? Or forty days and forty nights of rain? I'm sure Noah wasn't pleased with that one—and he had his prediction on pretty good authority.

Florida weather is probably the most unpredictable of all, but it you live here long enough you'll see some definite patterns emerge. It is hot in the summer. Sometimes it rains, and sometimes it doesn't. If it's a normal summer, it rains about the same time everyday. One year it may be 7 AM to 8 AM; the next year 3 PM to 4 PM.

There is usually one cold snap around Halloween. Then it's back to shorts and sandals until about Christmas. That is, if it doesn't get cold before. I've had the experience of wearing shorts and going barefoot on Christmas Day when the pipes froze the night before. No wonder thermostat switches take a beating here. I don't like January. It tends to be wet, cold and miserable (although this is our "dry season"). February is downright schizoid. The azaleas start blooming and everyone is thinking springtime—when suddenly arctic winds threaten limbs and lives. March and April can be cold or hot. Wearing a heavy coat on Easter is not unusual but you may as well drag out the bathing suit.

Do you know why nobody smells of mothballs in Florida?

It's because you can't safely pack anything away except that sweater made by Peruvians and purchased with the outside temperature at 10 degrees below. If you own a fur you may as well just give it to the cold storage people for what they'd charge for taking it out for you once or twice a year.

Pity the weatherman—don't malign him. He could have a nice, safe job up in Alaska. The fact that he is in Florida means that he is indeed brave—and radical.

Saving for a Rainy Day
April 1991

Rain is nice. It is so very wet. Sometimes I think I would have made a very good Noah and I am fairly sure my cats would have been cozy on the Ark. They'd each select a pile of newspapers or dirty laundry and curl up contentedly and sleep through the deluge. Dave would undoubtedly find some sort of tax return to dig into while I, well, I would watch it rain. This house is designed to keep a person indoors when it rains. The roof pattern shoots the water directly into the center of any stairwell coming or going. I have three sets of stairs and they are all so diabolically arranged! I do a lot of rain watching.

Dave only last week suggested we turn one of our yet unpurchased blue barrels into a rain barrel. How nice that would be on a day like today!

He would put a spigot on it and we could have watered our flower beds (and washed our hairs) with the real thing. (Maybe next year this time.) By the way, we found our barrels after a great deal of sleuthing just outside of Belleview at a bee keepers supply depot. No one will ever tell us what these barrels were originally used for, but they make dandy planters and rain barrels.

Rain has a bad name, but for the life of me I cannot understand why. No one gets cancer from too much rain. (We might, however, die of mold.) If we are wet enough we won't spontaneously combust. On the Fourth of July we pay lots of money to shoot fireworks into the sky and ooh and aah—then turn around and crawl under the bed when God displays His own fireworks in the Aprils and Mays and Septembers. A perverse lot we humans are! As a child, thunder was explained to me as St. Peter's Bowling League meeting. I can still see those white-bearded gents setting up the pins.

In defense of rain, I am adamant There is sometimes too much of a good thing: my mom once had clothes hanging on the line for two weeks—well-rinsed clothes. Reliant solely on a solar water heater, our family took cold baths or heated water over the stove in a pot. The river (Hillsborough, in Tampa) had overstepped its banks, the dam had broken for the umpteenth time, and lots of folks were pretty unhappy with the rains that came and came and came. For me, I looked at the greenest green this side of Seattle, Washington. When the sun finally came out (and we scraped the mildew from our bodies), the landscape was golden and pure and washed.

As a child I had no sympathy for those who chose to build homes in the flood plain. As an adult, I figure those are the risks one assumes when one chooses Florida—much as one would assume earthquakes in California or tornadoes in Kansas; snowstorms in Wisconsin or flash floods in Utah. I choose the magnificent thunderstorm. The snap crackle and pop and bang bang bang of the sky. I've lost two telephone answering machines to God's wonder; a VCR, one television and a thirty-seven page thesis that I hadn't saved on the computer to lightning. We have a tree out front right now that is evidence of a strike.

This then is Florida. Welcome to My World.

Rainy Day Woman
June 1992

Perhaps

it is because I'm a Florida person that rain is enchanting. When the barometric pressure goes up, my blood pressure goes down. Steel gray skies are so nice for a change. It is a look at the netherworld. It's a world of muffled barks and quiet cats. Birds don't chirp. A quiet curtain falls from the sky. Not even the wind whistles. It purrs. The air is a delicious blend of wet salt and tree smell.

It's a day when one doesn't have to feel guilty for not doing anything at all. It's the morning to sleep late—well past dawn—because you didn't see dawn at all. There is no insistent urge to shop or market or garden or beat rugs. (That particular urge doesn't happen very often even on sunny days.)

Rain is one of those things that people pray for. They also pray for it to stop. I've never understood this thinking. Noah may have had a bit of a problem with rain and I'll admit that when my new house was flooded, I was more than annoyed. I remember sliding down a mountainside in a sleeping bag in North Carolina in 1964, and another time when my children were tenting it outside the motorhome and banged on the door: "We're drowning!" "A little water never hurt little boys" I said but I let them in.

To me, there is a certain romance associated with rain. Cold rain is miserable but brings out the best in fellows. A man I hardly knew gave me his last pair of dry wool socks in the middle of a freezing rain when my boots were so soggy and my feet so cold. If I could, I would have bronzed those socks as a tribute to Paul—whatever his last name was.

There is Minnesota Rain. It drives itself across the Boundary Waters lakes at hurricane force and slams against a canoe like a sheet of plastic. Nothing is as cold as a Minnesota rain in June. There were five of us, all family. We pitched a tent in a hurry, dove in and made some Lipton's soup on a backpacking stove. Then, like puppies, we all flopped into a heap and slept in a cozy nest. Never before (and never since) had our family been such a huddled mass. If it hadn't been for that rain, one would be tossing a Frisbee, another fishing, and somebody else would be under a tree reading *War and Peace*.

Florida rains are probably the best. Except for our infrequent hurricanes, they are predictably unpredictable. Each summer sets its own pattern. To be a weatherman in Florida is almost as risky a job as being a police chief in Cedar Key. No one plans picnics or weddings or funerals around the weather. Rain? It will or it won't.

In case you are wondering, I am a transplant to Cedar Key. I grew up in the Hurricane Capital of the World: Tampa—in the days when it was normal to have two or three during the season. I've never had the responsibility as an adult of battening down the hatches or doing any or all of the things that need to be done to prepare. I may have to learn.

We moved to Cedar Key just after Hurricane Elena. Elena didn't even strike Cedar Key like I remember Tampa's storms, but there was damage. Lots of damage. Tampa had its Hillsborough River dam collapse more than once—flooding new, unprepared homes. We lived only a few blocks from the river but on relatively high ground. Even as a small child I knew and respected storms. I also liked the fact that I got out of school, the dim quiet of the house with candles and the excitement of eating from a Sterno stove. My brother and I were admonished not to go outside during the "eye" but we always did. There was a green glow to the world. Oaks had fallen. We were smart enough not to step on power lines. We felt the wind change and ran for the back door.

The second half of the storm meant it would be over soon. Our mom was often left with clothes drying on the line for weeks. It rained and rained and rained and you'd think that I would have hated it.

Rain banged against the windows. We brought the cats and dogs into the house. Daddy couldn't go to work. We played games by candlelight and kerosene lamps. No electricity, no phone, no pool, lots of pets.

Hurricane season is not over yet. The old days of coping are long gone. Now we have flood insurance and wind insurance and all kinds of things that weren't available in the 1940's. We know to listen to the warnings. Maybe we are a more careful population.

My suggestions for storm preparation are these (and I have been trained as a disaster nurse and worked in this capacity for "Elena"):

> Before anything happens, put in a supply of clean drinking water. Coolers, jars, bottles, anything. Fill a clean bathtub with water for flushing.
> Canned goods, with a non-electric can opener.
> Kerosene lamps or candles and be sure to keep kids away from these. Camp stoves are okay but again, caution with kids.
> Tie down anything in the yard that will be blown by wind—trash cans, boats, *anything*. A boat is much better off in water than it is at a dock. Anchor it securely out in deep water.

If asked to evacuate, evacuate. Lives are still more important than property.

Just a note here on my last suggestion: I do realize that there were problems in Cedar Key with evacuation during Elena. She was a most capricious storm and it was handled badly. I was manning an evacuation center in Orlando that weekend. Folks from St. Petersburg Beach were filing in on what was a relatively mild day in South West Orange County. I got the call at 4 AM and hied myself to the school evacuation center ASAP. Folks were really mad. The storm had moved north to Cedar Key by the time they evacuated. I coffeed and donutted them but I couldn't let them go back home because the bridge was closed. I couldn't let them bring inside their Weimerauners or their big black Labrador Retrievers. I spent my day trying to keep their kids from running up and down the bleachers at Oak Ridge High School gym. As a ham radio operator, I worked with the fellow who was doing the emergengy transmissions. This was serious business.

Rain is special. We don't need it in great globs or storms perhaps. But we need it. Storms raise the water table. Storms drench the foliage. Storms are nature's way of cleaning the trees. Storms give us time to pause, a reason to hug and get warm. Storms give us Puritan Americans a reason to snuggle and cuddle and coo.

Listen to the rain. Besides flooding your living room, it just might flood your heart.

Do Like They Do in Georgia... About the Weather, That Is
March 1993

What *do* they do about rain in Georgia? Why, they let it rain, of course ! The same can hold true for wind or flooding or drought, I suppose. Good advice from that purveyor of wisdom: my dad—back in the days when "hurricane" was a household Florida word, and everyone kept a supply of Sterno for cooking and the term "hurricane lamp" had real meaning. Bathtubs were Cloroxed and filled and entrenching tools were the commonest form of plumbing devices that worked. Everyone hoped that the roof wouldn't blow off, but sometimes it did. Then, everything got wet. There really wasn't much anyone could do about it except "do like they do in Georgia..."

Last week we were getting ready to bed down on a sand bar alongside the Suwannee River. The soft river breeze was enough to discourage the mosquitoes. The sun set gently behind wispy clouds. As the brilliant blue sky darkened into purple, the stars peeked through the curtain, winking at us. Soon the entire area was washed with the brilliant white light of the full moon. It wasn't hot and it wasn't cold. The sleeping bag was cozy but not confining. It was, in the fullest sense of the word, glorious! Morning dawned cool but not damp. Within an hour we were peeling our wind pants off to risk a pinkening skin.

The river was high and the current brisk. It was, most of the time, a lazy paddle downstream from Fargo, Georgia to Suwannee River State Park near Lake City, Florida—eighty-nine or so miles. One day was nicer than the other and the evenings were the nicest I've ever spent out of doors any place ever! (These days I'm spending almost as much time on the ground as I do under a roof!) "Why haven't we done this before?"

In five days on the river we saw a total of six people (until we approached the state park)—only two of those were in a boat on the river! What a River! It twists and turns, bubbles and rushes; it meanders among swamp and scrub; is bordered by limestone caverns; is overhung by massive oaks and cypress. Bluffs this time of year are pastel wonders: pink-gold of new maple growth, gray-green of cedar, chartreuse of new oak, rough saw-teeth of palmetto. Almost every inside curve is outlined with the white sugar sand associated with the upper Gulf Coast, broad expanses of beach, fringed with oak woods. The water is tawny-colored with the tannin from tree roots—looking all the world like a rich dark clear tea. Our canoes cut silent swaths as we imagined ourselves anytime back in time—far from the madding crowd.

Our companions—long time friends—are experienced outdoors-people but are more used to organized hunting parties and treks with professional guides. Dave and I have different experiences and had heard the nasty rumors that the weather was going to change. Wouldn't it be sad if we fooled Mother Nature and didn't have to use our Gore-tex rain suits? Let that heavy woolen sweater stay in the stuff sack?

We hauled the canoes out Friday afternoon. The temperature hovered around 85. My sunburn itched. We lashed the canoes to the top of our truck and headed back to Georgia to retrieve our friend's car from the parking lot of the Gator Motel. We ate ice cream and said our farewells—still exclaiming over the obscenely delicious (or was it deliciously obscene?) weather we'd had all week.

"Do you want to go home just now?"

"Let's spend the night in Valdosta. Tomorrow is Garage Sale Day."

It was clear by 5:30 AM that either Valdosta was having an earthquake, tornado or hurricane, or that we had been having simultaneous nightmares. We heard that trucks were all over I-75 and in the light of our canoe being on top of the truck, we opted for the less traveled US 41 heading home. Five miles out of Valdosta turned us around. Pine trees littered the road. Big Georgia Pines! I navigated us across the state line—no electricity in South Georgia or North Florida. The river that was so peaceful just the day before was now roiling.

We stopped at the Telford Hotel in White Springs:

"Are you serving breakfast?"

"Yes."

"Do you have electricity?"

"No."

The big dining room was lit with gas lamps. They couldn't make toast but the ham and eggs were just fine. Apologizing for the lack of cash register, the waitress just rounded our bill off to the nearest dollar—ignoring things like sales tax. Every time someone opened the outside door, oak leaves blew in and settled on the table—in our coffee—on our plates. (This was just like camping!)

We got as far as Chiefland before we realized what destruction this freak storm had caused right in our own backyard. Swarms of people were belly up to the registers at Wal-Mart and Winn-Dixie. Funny, on a Saturday afternoon, we saw not one person from Cedar Key in that store! (That should have told us something!) Bottled water, Coleman stoves and lanterns, kerosene were hot-selling items. We were well equipped to do without electricity or water. What we weren't prepared for was being told "you can't go home!" In situations like this where there just isn't anything we can do about it, we just think about it tomorrow. After spending the night in a Gainesville motel, tomorrow came.

Arriving in Cedar Key that morning, what we saw was a blow—no pun intended. It could have been worse—much worse! This is no solace to those friends who lost their homes or to those people who were faced with looking for their boats or yard furniture or pieces of new docks or roofs. It's no comfort to all the people who worked all day Sunday mopping out stores or trying to preserve food without electric power. It's no comfort to the terrified pets.

Today we are thanking God that it wasn't worse: the sun is shining and neighbor is helping neighbor. There's a spirit here that can't be denied. Nerves are frayed and folks are tired after the "No-Name Hurricane."

We can't really do much about the weather, but we can keep our own counsel: "Do like they do in Georgia..."

A Final Word

A Fine Farewell

Writing for the *Beacon* started as a lark, but ended in a five-year tenure. Those five years were years of minor celebrity status. I wrote about things I knew best and people who were unlikely to sue me for defamation of character: namely, my family, my cats and my editor. Dave called himself my "Fang," referring to the acerbic wit of Phyllis Diller toward her husband and foil. "You have a very funny wife," he was told on more than one occasion. His response: "She's pretty funny to live with, too." My style was less than reverent and one letter to our editor declared Dave to be a "Saint." He wouldn't live that title down: he had earned it.

During those years I was raked over the coals by the Antivivisectionist League of Philadelphia for graphically describing how my grandfather prepared the Sunday chicken dinner—from start to finish—of the chicken, at least. An aunt-in-!aw didn't like my poking fun at the deadly sins and my own mother suggested that my memory was faulty when I wrote about her keeping my baby teeth in a jar on the buffet until my children started asking about those "dinosaur bones." Writing about the cats was easier: they were always doing something cute or obnoxious, but whenever I did, I found yet another abandoned kitten on my doorstep. I enjoyed the fan mail and the folks who would never have introduced themselves otherwise. Heck, I was even sad for them when I quit writing the column.

My Last Letter to the Beacon
February 15, 2001

Mike Raftis—otherwise known as "Salty"—wrote a commentary for the Beacon called "Salty Sez." Admired for his politics by many, he caused the more liberal members of the community to cringe. He was a friend despite his opinions and we enjoyed "ragging" each other.

Dear Editor:

Anyone who reads the Cedar Key Beacon is aware of our publisher's (Michael Raftis') political stance. While some of us consider his views absurd, we honor his right to vent them. It is among the oldest traditions of newspapering that the publisher be slanted, biased and prejudiced. Look at the popular names of old newspapers: The Tallahassee Democrat, the Hamilton (Ohio) Republican. There were newspapers who took up the cause of abolition of slavery and civil rights; newspapers who espoused wars; newspapers who promoted the American Revolution (it was called sedition back then). Newspapers have sneered at women's suffrage and newspapers hailing the Chief Executive and some wanting to impeach him. This newspapering business is a private enterprise and the publisher (and sometimes the editor) calls the shots, set the tone; it's called "freedom of the press." Don't be too hard on Michael Raftis. He keeps this little newspaper going week after week, year after year, and is not getting rich off the endeavor. In between his musings and diatribes local people find out local news. He also gives you and me space to disagree with his politics in this reader forum. If it makes you feel better, not all of us believe that Ronald Reagan was one of our "greatest" presidents.

Susan Roquemore
Cedar Key, Florida

Susan Roquemore is a native of Tampa. She was born, not hatched—despite popular opinions to the contrary. She spent five years at the University of Florida collecting degrees and married a "saint." She and attorney husband David have three sons whom she declines to discuss (at the moment) for fear of child abuse charges: their ages are 30, 27 and 25. You will hear more about them later.

Susan is the author of essays and vignettes of everyday life: albeit her life is not always so "everyday." She wrote a weekly column "Impressions" for the Cedar Key Beacon for five years.

Her "stories" are about her "everyday existence" on the Appalachian Trail, of "coping" with "everyday" things like parents and children, and cats with hairballs. She'll tell you about the books she's reading at the moment and maybe (if you aren't lucky!) how she broke her leg in the Maine wilderness or "cured" a case of hives in a Cairo, Egypt hotel room and set a fellucca driver's arm on the same day she played chess with the minister from Oman. You'll learn that her secret passion is fine dining in odd places and her wish is to become some newspaper's "Mystery Diner."

When she isn't hiking, Susan lives in Cedar Key with husband David and her two cats, Shadow and Miss Petunia.

Robin Raftis
2001